Discover the
Northwestern Adirondacks

Four-Season Adventures through the
Boreal Forest and the Park's Frontier Region

Discover the Northwestern Adirondacks

Four-Season Adventures through the
Boreal Forest and the Park's Frontier Region

Barbara McMartin
Lee M. Brenning
Peter O'Shea

Prepared with the assistance of
Francis B. Rosevear and Anne L. Burnham

Backcountry Publications
Woodstock, Vermont

An Invitation to the Reader
Over time trails can be rerouted and signs and landmarks altered. If you find that changes have occurred on the routes described in this book, please let us know so that corrections may be made in future editions. The author and publisher also welcome other comments and suggestions. Address all correspondence to:

Editor
Discover the Adirondack Series
Backcountry Publications
P.O. Box 175
Woodstock, VT 05091

Library of Congress Cataloging-in-Publication Data

McMartin, Barbara.
 Discover the northwestern Adirondacks : four-season adventures through the boreal forest and the park's frontier region / Barbara McMartin, Lee M. Brenning, Peter O'Shea : prepared with the assistance of Francis B. Rosevear and Anne L. Burnham.
 p. cm. — (Discover the Adirondacks series : 8)
 Includes bibliographical references.
 ISBN 0-942440-48-X :
 1. Outdoor recreation—New York (State)—Adirondack Park—Guide -books. 2. Adirondack Park (N.Y.)—Description and travel—Guide -books. I. Brenning, Lee M., 1955- . II. O'Shea, Peter V. III. Title. IV. Series.
GV191.42.N7M34 1990
917.47′5′0443—dc20   89-29906
                                                     CIP

© 1990 by Barbara McMartin
All rights reserved
Published by Backcountry Publications, Inc.
A division of The Countryman Press, Inc.
Woodstock, Vermont 05091

Printed in the United States of America by McNaughton & Gunn
Typesetting by Sant Bani Press
Series design by Leslie Fry
Layout by Barbara McMartin
Trail overlays by VLS Designs

Photograph Credits
Lee M. Brenning, cover, 2, 36, 43, 46, 52, 56, 61, 63, 64, 67, 71, 106, 118, 137, 141, 147, 149, 151, 156, 159, 161, 163, 166, 168, 170, 173, 176
Anne L. Burnham, 20, 23, 26, 72, 77, 81, 82, 184, 186, 196, 198, 212
Barbara McMartin, 6, 204, 207
Ruth Rosevear, 95

Photographs
Cover: *Channel leading to Bog Lake*
Page 2: *Bassout Pond*
Page 6: *View from the top of Lampson Falls*

Acknowledgments

This book has benefited more from the careful research of Francis B. Rosevear than any other book in the *Discover* series. We thank him for all the work he has done for the series as well as for the special care he has given to accounts of his favorite destinations, the survey markers in the Five Ponds area and the "Dagger." We are indebted to him for his historical research and careful reading of much of the text.

We were indeed fortunate to have Anne L. Burnham photograph so many of the places described by Peter O'Shea. Her many hours of work and her fine, artistic eye bring carefully planned views of many hard-to-reach places.

Rangers and foresters in the Department of Environmental Conservation Region 6 have been most helpful. Among them were Rangers Howard Graham of Pitcairn; Joseph Kennedy of Tupper Lake (Bog River Flow); Terry Perkins, Stillwater; Assistant Forest Ranger John Harrington, Long Lake (Lake Lila); and Senior Forester Scott Grey. A special thanks also is due John Kramer, associate forester in the Canton office, who helped all three authors.

Peter benefited greatly from stories of wildlife and trapping told by Red Johnson, a longtime woodsman and trapper.

Lee gives thanks to Georgie for important field support, so welcome on the journeys deep into the wilderness that were necessary for the research for this guide.

Barbara received important assistance from Gerold Pepper, Librarian of the Adirondack Museum, who found answers to many puzzling questions. The Adirondack Museum Library has been a great help throughout the entire *Discover* series.

Barbara's husband, W. Alec Reid, printed the black and white photographs used in this guide, as well as almost all of those used in the rest of the *Discover* series. The many hours spent in the dark room represent a real labor of love.

To all those who helped with this guide, we offer a heartfelt thanks.

Contents

Introduction

THIS GUIDE COVERS a region that is the Adirondacks' last frontier. Most of its forests were not discovered and logged until the end of the nineteenth century. Many places remained to be exploited in this century. And, as the current wave of harvest is ending, many tracts are being sold to the state or opened to the public via easements. Although this guide covers lands that have been owned by the state for many years, it introduces a number of tracts that are just now open to the public—new frontiers of recreation.

This remote corner of the Adirondacks is far from all but a few centers of population. The region has no tall mountains, and only a few small mountains with views. It has many lakes and ponds and more miles of navigable rivers than any other portion of the park. Eskers from glacial rivers weave throughout the region, their steep slopes cloaked in hemlock and pine. Cut through soils of sand and gravel deposited by the glaciers, the region's often sluggish rivers course slowly through the deep forests.

These attributes do not describe what is unique about the northwestern Adirondacks—its boreal forests, even though the waters and glaciers provide for the presence of the forests. Boreal stands, largely spruce, with tamarack and cedar, grow in the bogs and wet places that are relics of glacial ponds. These forests have been the last great source of softwoods in the park. They are home to varieties of wildlife that thrive only in boreal regions; spruce grouse and moose are found in larger populations than elsewhere in the park. The elusive Canada jay and the arctic three-toed woodpecker are found only in these boreal forests. Loons breed on most lakes and ponds. To maintain this wildlife by preserving these ecologically distinct boreal habitats has been the motivating force behind the state's acquisition of so many tracts within the northwestern Adirondacks.

A glance at the map shows that there is a greater proportion of private lands here than in most corners of the park. Until recently this has limited recreation to the Five Ponds Wilderness Area, the Cranberry Lake Wild Forest, and a few isolated parcels. Recent acquisitions have added the Wilderness Lakes Tract to the west of Five Ponds. Watson's East Triangle now completes the contiguous stretch of state land all the way to Aldrich Wild Forest. An adjacent tract, once owned by Diamond International, has recently been acquired by the state.

Several years ago, the state acquired part of Nehasane Preserve around Lake Lila, which lies on the eastern boundary of the region. Lands around the Bog River have been added; they reach all the way west to the Five Ponds Wilderness, opening up a canoe route that had been closed to the public since the late nineteenth century, and consolidating what may one day be the Adirondacks' largest wilderness area.

A wonderful new recreation area has been created around the Grass River near the park's boundary. In fact, fully one-third of the destinations described in this guide were closed to the public just a decade ago.

The northwestern Adirondacks have always been the realm of sportsmen, most recently deer hunters. The amount of private land where timber and pulpwood are harvested assures that this will remain the province of hunters for a long time to come. But others are discovering this last frontier of recreation—hiking on long trails, bushwhacking in true wilderness, canoeing quiet streams, skiing broad, abandoned logging roads, and camping on remote lakes and ponds.

How to Use the Discover Guides

The regional guides in the *Discover the Adirondacks* series will tell you enough about each area so that you can enjoy it in many different ways at any time of year. Each guide will acquaint you with that region's access roads and trailheads, its trails and unmarked paths, some bushwhack routes and canoe trips, and its best picnic spots, campsites, and ski-touring routes. At the same time, the guides will introduce you to valleys, mountains, cliffs, scenic views, lakes, streams, and myriad other natural features.

Some of the destinations are within walking distance of the major highways that ring the areas, while others are miles deep into the wilderness. Each description will enable you to determine the best excursion for you to enjoy the natural features you will pass, whether you are on a summer day hike or a winter ski-touring trek. The sections are grouped in chapters according to their access points. Each chapter contains a brief introduction to that area's history and the old settlements and industries that have all but disappeared into the wilderness. Throughout the guide you will find accounts of the geological forces that shaped features of the land, mention of unusual wildflowers, and descriptions of forest stands.

It is our hope that you will find this guide not only an invitation to know and enjoy the woods but a companion for all your adventures there.

MAPS AND NOMENCLATURE

The *Adirondack Atlas*, a map published by City Street Directory of Poughkeepsie, New York, is the best reference for town roads, and it has the added advantage of identifying state land. In spite of the fact that it has not been updated to show recent acquisitions, it is a valuable aid where public and private lands are intricately mixed. The new *Adirondack North Country Regional Map* shows all state land, including purchases made through 1986. Copies may be obtained free of charge as long as the supply lasts by contacting Adirondack North Country Association, P.O. Box 148, Saranac Avenue, Lake Placid, NY 12946, phone 518-523-9820.

This guide contains maps showing all the routes mentioned and are adequate for the marked trails. You may still want to carry the USGS (United States Geological Survey) topographic quadrangle sheets for the region, and you ought to have them for the more difficult bushwhacks. However, much of this area has recently been resurveyed by the USGS and new maps will be available in a couple of years. The new maps, in a larger scale than the current 15-minute series, will be most welcome.

The guide uses a combination of USGS maps and those from the New York State Department of Transportation (DOT), which are 7.5-minute maps prepared from the old 15-minute USGS surveys. The maps used: Hermon, West Pierrepont, Albert Marsh, Rainbow Falls, Sylvan Falls, Carry Falls Reservoir, Childwold, Brother Ponds, Tooley Pond, DeGrasse, Fine, Oswegatchie, Newton Falls, Cranberry Lake, Long Tom Mtn., Piercefield, Little Tupper Lake, Sabattis, Wolf Mtn., Five Ponds, Oswegatchie SE, Oswegatchie SW, Remington Corners, Soft Maple Reservoir, Stillwater, Beaver River, Nehasane Lake, Brandreth Lake, Number Four, Stark, Stillwater Mtn.

Maps are available locally in many sporting goods stores. You can order maps from USGS Map Distribution Branch, Box 25286, Denver Federal Center, Denver, CO 80225. Maps are more easily obtained from a private source, Timely Discount Topos. You can call them at 1-800-821-7609 to place an order. They will send the maps the day after they receive your check or money order. All maps purchases through Timely Discount are on a prepaid basis only; they do not accept credit cards.

This guide uses the spellings given in the USGS, but local variations are noted.

DISTANCE AND TIME

Distance along the routes is measured from the USGS survey maps and is accurate to within ten percent. It is given in miles, feet, or yards except where local signs use metric measure. Distance is a variable factor in comparing routes along paths or bushwhacks. Few hikers gauge distance accurately even on well-defined trails.

Time is given as an additional gauge for the length of routes. This provides a better understanding of the difficulty of the terrain, the change of elevation, and the problems of finding a suitable course. Average time for walking trails is 2 miles an hour, 3 miles if the way is level and well-defined; for paths, 1½ to 2 miles an hour; and for bushwhacks, 1 mile an hour.

Vertical rise usually refers to the change in elevation along a route up a single hill or mountain; *elevation change* generally refers to the cumulative change in elevation where a route crosses several hills or mountains.

A line stating distance, time, and vertical rise or elevation change is given with the title of each section describing trails and most paths, but not for less distinct paths and bushwhacks for which such information is too variable to summarize. Distance and times are for *one way only*, unless otherwise stated. The text tells you how to put together several routes into longer treks that will occupy a day or more.

TYPES OF ROUTES

Each section of this guide generally describes a route or a place. Included in the descriptions are such basic information as the suitability for different levels of woods experience, walking (or skiing, paddling, and climbing) times, distances, directions to the access, and, of course, directions along the route itself. The following definitions clarify the terms used in this book.

A route is considered a *trail* if it is so designated by the New York State Department of Environmental Conservation (DEC). This means the trail is routinely cleared by DEC or volunteer groups and adequately marked with official DEC disks. *Blue disks* generally indicate major north-south routes, *red disks* indicate east-west routes, and *yellow disks* indicate side trails. This scheme is not, however, applied consistently throughout the Adirondacks.

Some trails have been marked for *cross-country skiing*, and new *pale yellow disks with a skier* are used. *Large orange disks* indicate *snowmobile trails*, which are limited to some portions of Wild Forest Areas. Snowmobiles are permitted on them in winter when there is sufficient snow cover. The guide indicates those trails not heavily used where skiing and snowmobiling may be compatible, but a skier must always be cautious on a snowmobile trail. Hikers can enjoy both ski and snowmobile trails.

A *path* is an informal and unmarked route with a clearly defined foot tread. These traditional routes, worn by fishermen and hunters to favorite spots, are great for hiking. A path, however, is not necessarily kept open, and fallen trees and new growth sometimes obliterate its course. The paths that cross wet meadows or open fields often become concealed by lush growth. You should always carry a map and compass when you are following an unmarked path and you should keep track of your location.

There is a safe prescription for walking paths. In a group of three or more hikers, stringing out along a narrow path will permit the leader to scout until the path disappears, at which point at least one member of the party should still be standing on an obvious part of the path. If that hiker remains standing while those in front range out to find the path, the whole group can continue safely after a matter of moments.

Hikers in the north country often use the term *bushwhack* to describe an uncharted and unmarked trip. Sometimes bushwhacking literally means pushing brush aside, but it usually connotes a variety of cross-country walks.

Bushwhacks are an important part of this regional guide series because of the shortage of marked trails throughout much of the Adirondack Park and the abundance of little-known and highly desirable destinations for which no visible routes exist. Although experienced bushwhackers may reach these destinations with not much more help than the knowledge of their location, I think most hikers will appreciate these simple descriptions that point out the easiest and most interesting routes and the possible pitfalls. In general, descriptions for bushwhacks are less detailed than those for paths or trails; it is assumed that those who bushwhack have a greater knowledge of the woods than those who walk only marked routes.

Bushwhack is defined as any trip through the woods without a trail, path, or the visible foot tread of other hikers, and without markings, signs, or blazes. It also means you will make your way by following a route chosen on a contour map, aided by a compass, using streambeds, valleys, abandoned roads, and obvious ridges as guides. Most bushwhacks require navigating by both contour map and compass, and an understanding of the terrain.

Bushwhack distances are not given in precise tenths of a mile. They are estimates representing the shortest distance one could travel between points. This reinforces the fact that each hiker's cross-country route will be different, yielding different mileages.

A bushwhack is said to be *easy* if the route is along a stream, a lakeshore, a reasonably obvious abandoned roadway, or some similarly well-defined feature. A short route to the summit of a hill or a small mountain can often be easy. A bushwhack is termed *moderate* if a simple route can be defined on a contour map and followed with the aid of a compass. Previous experience is necessary. A bushwhack is rated *difficult* if it entails a complex route, necessitating advanced knowledge of navigation by compass and reading contour maps and land features.

Compass directions are given in degrees from magnetic north and in degrees from true north. The text will usually specify which reference is used, but if no reference is given, the degrees refer to *magnetic north.*

The guide occasionally refers to old *blazed* lines or trails. The word "blaze" comes from the French *blesser* and means to cut or wound. Early loggers and settlers made deep slashes in good-sized trees with an axe to mark property lines and trails. Hunters and fishermen have also often made slashes with knives and, though they are not as deep as axe cuts, they can still be seen. *It is now, and has been for many years, illegal to deface trees in the Forest Preserve in this manner.* Following an old blazed path for miles in dense woods is often a challenging but good way to reach a trailless destination.

You may see *yellow paint daubs on a line of trees,* also referred to in the text as paint blazes. These lines usually indicate the boundary between private and public lands. Individuals have also used different colors of paint to mark informal routes from time to time. Although it is not legal to mark trails on state land, this guide does refer to such informally marked paths.

All *vehicular traffic,* except snowmobiles on their designated trails, is *prohibited* in the Forest Preserve. Vehicles are allowed on town roads and some roads that pass through state land to reach private inholdings. These roads are described in the guide, and soon the DEC will start marking those old roads that are open to vehicles. Most old roads referred to here are town or logging roads that were abandoned when the land around them became part of the Forest Preserve. Now they are routes for hikers, not for vehicles.

There has been an increase in the use of three- and four-wheeled off-road vehicles, even on trails where such use is prohibited. New laws have gone a long way toward stopping this in the Forest Preserve, ensuring that some of the old roads remain attractive hiking routes.

Cables have been placed across many streams by hunters and other sportsmen to help them cross in high water. The legality of this practice has been challenged. Some may be quite safe to use; others are certainly questionable. Using them is not a recommended practice, so when this guide mentions crossing streams to reach some of the hikes, you are urged to do so only when a boat can be used or when you can wade across in low water.

The *beginning of each section describing a trail* gives a summary of the distance, time, and elevation change for the trail. For unmarked routes, such information is given only within the text of each section—partly to allow for the great variations in the way hikers approach an unmarked route, and partly to emphasize the difficulty of those routes.

Protecting the Land

Most of the land described in these guides is in the Forest Preserve, land set aside a century ago. No trees may be cut on this state land. All of it is open to the public. The Adirondack Park Agency has responsibility for the Wilderness, Primitive, and Wild Forest guidelines that govern use of the Forest Preserve. Care and custody of these state lands is left to the Department of Environmental Conservation, which is in the process of producing Unit Management Plans for the roughly 130 separate Forest Preserve areas.

Camping is permitted throughout the public lands except at elevations above 4000 feet and within 150 feet of water or 100 feet of trails. In certain fragile areas, camping is restricted to specific locations, and the state is using a new No Camping disk to mark fragile spots. *Permits* for camping on state lands are needed only for stays that exceed three days or for groups of more than ten campers. Permits can be obtained from the local rangers, who are listed in the area phone books under New York State Department of Environmental Conservation.

Only dead and downed wood may be used for *campfires*. Build fires at designated fire rings or on rocks or gravel, and only when absolutely necessary; carry a small stove for cooking. Fire is dangerous and can travel rapidly through the duff or organic soil, burning roots and spreading through the forest. Douse fires with water, and be sure they are completely out and cold before you leave.

Private lands are generally not open to the public, though some individuals have granted public access across their land to state land. It is always wise to ask before crossing private lands. Be very respectful of private landowners so that public access will continue to be granted. Never enter private lands that have been posted unless you have the owner's permission. Unless the text expressly identifies an area as state-owned Forest Preserve or private land whose owner permits unrestricted public passage, the inclusion of a walk description in this guide does not imply public right-of-way.

Burn combustible trash and carry out everything else.

Most *wildflowers and ferns* mentioned in the text are protected by law. Do not pick them or try to transplant them.

Safety in the Woods

It is best *not to walk alone.* Make sure someone knows where you are heading and when you are expected back.

Carry water or other liquids with you. Not only are the mountains dry, but the recent spread of *Giardia* makes many streams suspect. I have an aluminum fuel bottle especially for carrying water; it is virtually indestructible and has a deep screw that prevents leaking.

Carry a small *day pack* with insect repellent, flashlight, first aid kit, emergency food rations, waterproof matches, jackknife, whistle, rain gear, and a wool sweater, even for summer hiking. Wear layers of wool and waterproof clothing in winter and carry an extra sweater and socks. If you plan to camp, consult a good outfitter or a camping organization for the essentials. Better yet, make your first few trips with an experienced leader or with a group.

Always carry a *map and compass.* You may also want to carry an altimeter to judge your progress on bushwhack climbs.

Wear *glasses* when bushwhacking. The risk to your eyes of a small protruding branch makes this a necessity.

Carry *binoculars* for birding as well as for viewing distant peaks.

Use great care near the *edges of cliffs* and when *crossing streams* by hopping rocks in the streambed. Never bushwhack unless you have gained a measure of woods experience. If you are a novice in the out-of-doors, join a hiking group or hire the services of one of the many outfitters in the north country. As you get to know the land, you can progress from the standard trails to the more difficult and more satisfyingly remote routes.

Bears have become a problem throughout the Adirondacks in areas where campers have concentrated. Since you will have to camp to reach many of the distant points in this guide, you should be aware of ways to discourage bears. In the past, bears have been an especially bad problem at such popular places as High Falls on the Oswegatchie.

Keep all food in sealed containers and hang all food overnight in "bear bags," suspended on a rope thrown between two trees at least 15 feet apart, with the bear bag at least 10 feet from the ground. Do not keep food in your tent. Bears have learned that campers have food. No bears have attacked bear bags in this region, but at least one clever bear in the park has learned to break the ropes holding bear bags, so make sure your bags are secured high enough not to attract attention. And, in one region of the park, rangers caution that campers should not sleep in clothing they wear when cooking. It may be wise to suspend your pack as well.

Bears are not a problem during the daytime and only at night if they detect food. If bears do come near your campsite, clanging pots and pans may scare them away.

Horseshoe Lake Wild Forest

PARALLELING THE SOUTHWESTERN boundary of this guide is the Adirondack Division of the New York Central Railroad, which opened the region to logging and to settlement by vast estates. The sale of large portions of these estates to the state and the acquisition by the state of the right-of-way of the railroad have brought many new recreational opportunities in areas that have long been closed to the public.

Construction of the railroad was begun in 1891 by Dr. William Seward Webb, son-in-law of William H. Vanderbilt. It was called Webb's folly, but soon became known as the Golden Chariot Route. Completed in a remarkably short time, the railroad would have hooked up in Tupper Lake with Hurd's Northern Adirondack Line from Moira, but Hurd did not cooperate, so Webb ran his line to Malone instead. That Remsen to Malone Branch (or Mohawk and Malone Branch, as it became known) was completed in 1892. Pushed north from Old Forge, the railroad enters the area of this guide at Beaver River, a station on the south shore of Stillwater Reservoir. Next is the station of Little Rapids on the Beaver River. Dr. Benjamin Brandreth purchased all of Township 39, a tract of 26,000 acres which is owned to this day by his descendants. Feeder lines from the station at Brandreth brought timber to market from the Brandreth estate. Webb's Nehasane Preserve, centered around Lake Lila, had three stations on the railroad. After passing Robinwood at Bog Lake and the Whitney Estate, tracts that remain private, the line goes through stations that all figure as starting points of adventures described in this and other chapters. The railroad went through Sabattis ("Long Lake West" station), across the Bog River, and on to Horseshoe, the station built by A. Augustus Low. Next came Childwold, the site of the Childwold Park House hotel, where the Grasse River Railroad branched west toward the Grass River. The main line crossed the Raquette River at Piercefield and finally reached Tupper Lake Junction and the Hurd Railroad, which figures in so many adventures in *Discover the Northern Adirondacks*.

West Branch Oswegatchie

While the railroad, large estates, logging, and fires are motifs that thread through many excursions, the state's strong policy of acquisition remains the most important theme—for without it, most of the adventures in this corner of the northwestern Adirondacks would not be open to the public. We start with visits to the Horseshoe Lake Wild Forest and three blocks recently acquired on its southeastern boundary.

1 Bog River Falls and the Lower Bog River
Picnicking, canoeing, fishing, river amble, wildlife, maps I and II

The Bog River flows into Big Tupper Lake over a two-tiered waterfall that tumbles under a stone bridge to drop abruptly into the lake. The DEC has an informal day-use area here with picnic tables nestled under the hemlocks and pines. From here there are several pleasant options: canoeing the lower Bog River, hiking old overgrown paths that parallel the river for intimate glimpses of it (sections 4 and 5), and canoeing into Big Tupper Lake.

NY 421 heads west from NY 30, 9 miles south of the junction of NY 3 and 30 in Tupper Lake, 13.4 miles north of the junctions of NY 28N and 30 in Long Lake. From NY 30, it's 0.75 mile along NY 421 to the bridge over the Bog River. On the way to the bridge, you pass a handsome stone colonial house, built at the turn of the century by Roswell Flower, a former governor of New York and a north country native.

To canoe the Lower Bog River, put in on the right bank above the falls and head upriver for about 2 miles along the quiet water to the first rapids, where there is a landing to the left on the southwestern shore. From this point it is 5 miles to Low's Lower Dam, a magnificent, yet vexing, series of rapids, riffles, and occasional small waterfalls best left to whitewater enthusiasts. The dark brown color of the water reflects tannic acid of the headwater bogs.

2 Tupper Lake
Canoeing, camping, fishing, maps I and II

Much of the western shore of "Big" Tupper Lake is Forest Preserve. The lake stretches from the foot of Bog River Falls to the outskirts of the village

Looking over Bog River Falls toward Tupper Lake

of Tupper Lake. The lake has the dual distinction of being fed by two rivers—the Bog and the Raquette—and of having a range of depths that supports a two-tiered fishery. Its deepest pools remain cold enough for lake and brook trout to breed and its shallows warm enough to support northern pike and walleye. Tupper has a surface area second only to Cranberry in this part of the park.

Driving along NY 30, you have glimpses of its rocky, cliff-faced western shores. You can explore the lake from its southern terminus at Bog River Falls or from a DEC boat launching site on the east shore near the northern end.

If you put in below Bog River Falls, you can more easily explore the Forest Preserve lands, which are concentrated at the southern end of the seven-mile-long lake. On the first 1.5 miles of western shoreline, there are the dilapidated buildings of the historic Veterans' Mountain Camp, which was established after World War I to cater to and rehabilitate veterans who were injured in that war. It has been closed for more than a decade and has been sold to a private developer.

About 2.5 miles from the put-in, there is a DEC lean-to on the shores of Black Bay, though its charming location means it is usually occupied. It is a good place for a base camp to explore the surrounding forest, which is quite wild as you leave the shoreline. A second secluded bay, about 0.5 mile north of the lean-to, has a trail leading from it for 0.3 mile to Bridge Brook Pond, a long arc-shaped pond that stretches northwest almost to Mount Arab. The pond has excellent brook trout fishing.

Map I: Sections 1-3
Based on NY State DOT 7½' Piercefield
Quadrangle.

- – – – Trail
———— Road
⊐⊏ Bridge
π Shelter
Ⓟ Parking

0   0.5   1.0 mile

2

1

Also shown on Map II

NY 421

Picnic Area

The eastern shores have several campsites on state lands, located on headlands topped by towering white and red pine. The DEC launch site, adjacent to NY 30 and 0.5 mile south of the metal bridge spanning the Raquette River, is ideal for probing the northern reaches of the lake. From here you can also ascend the Raquette River to Axton and Raquette Falls (see *Discover the High Peaks Adirondacks*). The rich marshes that surround the river continue into the northern portions of Tupper Lake. These marshes are breeding grounds for blue heron, bittern, Virginia and sora rails, blue-wing teal, and marsh hawks. There is little Forest Preserve land in the northern portion of the lake and all the islands are private; still, it is a great place for birding.

3 Mount Arab

Trail to a manned fire tower
0.8 mile, ½ hour, 740-foot vertical rise, map I

A short, very easy climb leads to the Mount Arab fire tower, which is manned from April through October. The mountain and its tower are beacons in the mostly rolling countryside that stretches west of Tupper Lake.

To reach the trailhead, take NY 3 for 4 miles west from Tupper Lake to Conifer Road and head left, south, on it for 1.8 miles to Eagle Crag Lake Road. Turn left on Eagle Crag Lake Road for 0.9 mile to the trailhead on the left.

The steady climb to the top starts through recently logged lands and continues through a ring of spruce that encircles the mountain just below the summit. There is a cabin in the fire-scarred clearing beside the tower. No camping is permitted in the clearing, but there is state land and a primitive campsite just over the crest beyond the tower.

From the tower you can see Tupper Lake Village with Ampersand Mountain looming in the distance beyond. Mount Matumbla lies to the north. South are the seemingly endless stretches of forested ridges and intervening streams and rivers. The flatland of marshes, bogs, peatland, and swamps spreads out to the far west and north, punctuated by lakes and ponds and meandering rivers.

Bog River Falls

4 Bog River Amble
Path, wildlife, snowshoeing, map II

Old logging roads in the Bog River's lower corridor lead to vantage points above the river, whose banks are thickly covered with spruce, fir, hemlock, and occasional white pine. The corridor, for several miles upriver from the falls, is an important deer wintering yard and attracts packs or families of the large eastern coyote that feed on the deer.

A gated jeep road heads left from NY 421, 0.2 mile north of the intersection of NY 421 and 30. The road reaches the Bog in 0.2 mile and crosses it on a cement bridge. Turn left across the river. The old road gradually becomes overgrown, succumbing to blowdown and disuse. When it becomes too dense, after a mile and a half or so, turn around, sometimes enjoying glimpses of cliffs over the river that you may miss on the way in.

5 Bog River from NY 30
Path, river views, map II
1.4 miles

An unmarked path leads from NY 30 through the recently acquired Goodman property to the Bog River. It begins on the west side of NY 30, 0.2 mile south of the intersection of NY 421 and 30, where a DEC sign warns that there is no motorized access. The path proceeds through a mostly mixed forest to climb a low hill and then gradually descends to the river. At 1 mile, you first see the river through a canopy of mature yellow birch. A landing at 1.2 miles is the end of the Lower Bog River Canoe trip (section 1).

The path continues for another 0.2 mile to end at the boundary of Forest Preserve lands. On the way it passes the confluence of the Bog River and Round Lake Outlet, branches of about equal size. Round Lake, 2 miles upriver, is heavily posted.

6 Horseshoe Lake
Camping, canoeing, fishing, map II

A large, isolated lake, almost entirely in the Forest Preserve, is located 4.7 miles from NY 30 on NY 421. It seems a world apart from nearby Tupper Lake, with almost no motorboats. Beyond the bridge over the Bog River, NY 421 follows the west shore of Tupper Lake, makes a sharp left turn at 1.6 miles, and heads west to the lake. The road follows the lake's southern shore, where there are numbered campsites, some with picnic tables and fire rings, many of them sheltered by the large hemlock that grace this shore. There are a couple of private inholdings along this shore, small tracts. Otherwise you can stop at one of the picnic sites and launch your canoe for several hours of exploring the lake's two deep bays.

Pavement ends at 5.7 miles; at 5.9 miles the road to Trout Pond and the Lower Dam forks left. The old Horse Shoe Station on the Adirondack Division Railroad—a replica of the Garden City, Long Island Station—built by A. A. Low, stood on the lake's western shore, 6.6 miles along the road. After crossing the railroad, the road makes a sharp turn to the left and ends at a gate at 7.3 miles. The continuing roadway may be driven by

Map II: Sections 1-2, 4-12
Based on NY State DOT, the Long Tom
Mountain, Piercefield, Sabattis and Little Tupper
Lake Quadrangles.

Trail
Path
Bridge
Shelter
Bushwhack
Scenic Views
Canoe Route
Parking

N

0   0.5   1.0 mile

Sardine Pond

Stone Pond

Silver Lake Mtn

Little Pine Pond

Gate
P
Horseshoe
BM 1738
Horseshoe
6   1727
Lake

Hitchins Bog

Old Road

8

10

11   Gate

N

12

7

Camps

RIVER
P

PIERCEFIELD

Snowmobile and Ski Route

Little Trout Pond

Trout Pond

DEC personnel and owners of the private inholdings along it, but it is open only to hiking by the public. This is where the walk to Low's Upper Dam (section 8) begins.

7 Adirondack Division Railroad
Snowmobile trail, cross-country skiing, maps II and III

In spite of the fact that several trestles are out and there is considerable beaver flooding, a 5.4-mile stretch of the railroad bed from Horseshoe Lake to Sabbatis can be skied. If time allows, the trip can be extended another 7 miles to Lake Lila (section 15) with the first portion of the way south of Sabbatis passing through private land.

The 11-mile road from NY 30 to Sabbatis is plowed irregularly in winter. NY 421 is plowed to within 0.7 mile of the railroad crossing.

The rail line goes southwest through a forest of emerging conifers with remnants of the original birch-aspen forest that pioneered this area that was so ravaged by the 1908 fires. After 0.5 mile, you see a portion of Hitchins Bog on your right. A trestle takes you over the Bog River and from it you have a great view across Hitchins Pond to the Bog River Cliffs. This is just before the midway point in the trip to Sabbatis. Wooden mileposts, delineating the mileage from the start of the line in Remsen, are still in place.

The Bog River and Lows Lake

MOST MID-NINETEENTH CENTURY paddlers visiting the Tupper Lake region were content to restrict their travels to the easily navigable Raquette River, forsaking the lake's other major tributary, the Bog River. Entering the lake at its southern end, the Bog River was the haunt of a few hardy trappers and hermits. Writers of the time who journeyed up to its headwaters told of an arduous trip through snag-filled channels and dismal pond chains to an area of forbidding, prehistoric solitude. Joel T. Headley, in *The Adirondack or, Life in the Woods*, describes ". . . a wilderness probably never trodden by human foot . . . " and a scene of ". . . indescribable loneliness. . . ." S. H. Hammond echoed these sentiments in *Wild Northern Scenes*, writing, ". . . so gloomy is the place, so sepulchral, such an air of desolation all around, that it brings over the mind a strong feeling of sadness and gloom. . . ." In such a place, it is easy to imagine the true beasts of the boreal wilderness making their last stand, and indeed, many tales of the taking of the "last moose in the Adirondacks" originate in the upper Bog River basin.

All this changed when Abbot Augustus Low, a wealthy partner in a prosperous New York City shipping and importing business, was charmed by the Adirondacks. Like his contemporary, William Seward Webb, he undertook an aggressive series of purchases of forested lands in the late nineteenth century that eventually totalled over 40,000 acres—most of the Bog River drainage. Staying first at a summer home on Bog Lake, he built a permanent home in 1900 on Silver Lake to the north which he had renamed Lake Marian after his wife. Not happy with the station at Horseshoe Lake, he replaced it with his own, and from it built his Horseshoe Forestry Company Railway, consisting of three branches, in 1897. In 1903, a dam was built, across the river at a point just over 7 miles from Tupper Lake, to supply power to the various operations Low was developing. He built a sawmill at Hitchins Pond, one of the first to use a band saw for processing lumber. He shipped "Virgin Forest Spring" water from a spring near the railroad to distant cities. He pioneered the use of tubing to collect maple sap in one of the most sophisticated sugaring operations in the east. His estate even produced berry preserves.

In 1907, Low had a second dam built three miles farther upstream, above Hitchins Pond. These points are now officially known as Low's Lower Dam and Low's Upper Dam, respectively.

In 1908, fires swept through a large portion of Low's holdings, greatly damaging the forest resource. Records show that his railway stopped running in 1911, but other operations continued. Many prominent acquaintances visited the Low estate in the first few decades of the twentieth century and among the political luminaries invited for hunting and fishing was Albany Mayor Erastus Corning, who stayed at the lodge on Bog Lake. Parcels of the estate were sold off through the years and in 1965, two years after his son's death, the remaining lands were sold to the Boy Scouts.

The Bog River was now quite different and its once forbidding course had become a smooth waterway between the dams. Above Low's Upper Dam, the flow gradually widened into the large impoundment now known as Lows Lake. Mud Lake was submerged, as were the channels to Bog Lake and Grass Pond. Navigation of the system was radically simplified, but private ownership and occupation presented different barriers to the traveling public. Until recently, you could paddle between the dams, but getting permission to carry around the upper dam was an exhaustive process, thus extended trips to the upper flow were for all practical purposes impossible. This changed in 1985, however, when the state acquired 9248 acres, adding most of the land surrounding the Bog River Flow to the Forest Preserve.

Despite the presence of the dams and the altered character of the flow, it remains a critical environmental area. With the adjoining Five Ponds Wilderness on the west, conditions are favorable to support the small group of moose returning to the area. The crags found on Grass Pond Mountain and nearby Graves Mountain provide excellent habitat for ravens and the returning golden eagle. This was also one of the last holdouts for the bald eagle in the Adirondacks and sightings in recent years signal its hopeful return. The flow now has one of the largest populations of breeding loons in the state and roughly thirty pairs rear their broods in the abundant bogs and marshes. Canada geese use the many bays and backwaters for stopovers during their migrations and several species of ducks are sure to be encountered along the way. Floating bogs occur in several locations and though some are stable enough to support trees, you should not attempt to walk on any of them, thus ensuring your safety and preventing damage to the mat vegetation.

The surrounding forest shows occasional signs of the natural and human impacts of the last century, but it has for the most part made a strong recovery. In the lowlands, aspen and birch have pioneered many of the fields left by fires and cutting. Other meadows have produced tall grasses and shrubs, creating the important "edge" habitat for many diverse species of woodland birds and mammals. On the upper slopes, recovery has been slow because of erosion and susceptibility to weather extremes, but this also provides good habitat for several species of raptors and high elevation plants. It's easy to see how such wise acquisitions benefit humans and wildlife.

8 Low's Upper Dam from Horseshoe Lake

Nature walk along old road, birding, cross-country skiing
2.6 miles, 1 hour, maps II and III

The gate at 7.3 miles marks the end of public use on the extension of NY 421 past Horseshoe Lake. You can park in a small turnoff on the right side. The road splits 0.1 mile beyond the barrier and you should turn left, passing through another gate. The right fork goes to private land around Lake Marian, Pine Pond, and beyond.

An expansive spruce and tamarack swamp lies between Horseshoe Lake and Hitchins Pond, and as you follow the road, Hitchins Bog, as it is called, soon appears on your left. This tract is entirely state owned and is a fascinating place. The lichen *usnea*, commonly known as old man's beard, hangs from the branches of many of the trees in shaggy grey-green strands. Poking up through the sphagnum understory are such acid-tolerant plants as trailing arbutus, leatherleaf, wintergreen, and creeping white winterberry. This is an excellent location to spot the elusive spruce grouse, who is right at home in this environment. Several other boreal species are also present, including grey jays, black-backed woodpeckers, and boreal chickadees.

After you pass the end of the swamp on the left, another, smaller swamp appears on your right. At 1.3 miles, a DEC sign tells you that you are entering the Bog River Area, and both sides of the road are now in the Forest Preserve. You pass a private jeep road forking right at 1.8 miles, near where Low's maple syrup evaporator was located.

At 2.6 miles, the route ends at another gate; straight ahead is the Upper Dam, which is described in section 10. The continuing roadway over the dam leads toward Sabattis and another private inholding. To the right is the road that led to the Boy Scout Camp. Also on the right, between buildings slated for removal, is the path to the Upper Dam Cliffs above Hitchins Pond (section 11).

Toad
Pond

Simmons
Pond

Olmstead
Pond

1689

(79)

Indian
Mountain

Indian Mountain
Pond
Indian Mountain
Pond

Also shown on Map XIII

(84)

Darn

(77)

(80)

Fishpole
Pond

ATE   FOREST   PRESERVE

Also shown on Map XIV

C L I F T O N

Ash
Pond

Cat Mtn
Pond

(74)

(78)

Cowhorn
Pond

Grass
Pond

Grass

(13)

Silver Leaf Pond

(81)

Halfmoon
Pond

Clear
Pond

Slender
Pond

High
Pond

Tamarack
Pond

(76)

O W S

(12)

ST. LAWRENCE CO.   STATE   FOREST   BOUNDARY

(82)

Put-in

(14)

Nicks
Pond

HAMILTON CO.
HERKIMER

Big Deer
Pond
1749

(70)

Tomar
Pond

(83)

Tomar
Mtn

A D I R O N D A C K   S T A T E   P

0   0.5   1.0 mile

S T A T E   F O R E S T   P R E S E R V E

N

Beaverdam

(62)

Map III. Sections 7-8, 12-14, 70, 74, 76-84
Based on NY State DOT 7½' Long Tom
Mountain, Sabattis and USGS 7½' Cranberry
Lake and Wolf Mountain Quadrangles.

- - - - Trail
— - — Path
· · · · Bushwhack
——— Canoe Route
Shelter
Bridge
Scenic View

Also shown on Map II

Hitchins Pond and the Lower Bog River Flow from the ridge above the pond

9 Low's Lower Dam and Trout Pond
Road and snowmobile trail
1.4-mile trail from the Lower Dam, map II

At 5.9 miles from NY 30, a side road turns left off NY 421 and leads to Low's Lower Dam, 0.8 mile away. The narrow, gravel road can be quite rough, though it is maintained and improvements are being made. You should be careful not to bottom out your vehicle. It is closed in winter and the mud season of early spring and does not reopen until dried out again, as late as mid-May. A parking area, register, signboard, and gate are located 100 feet before the dam and since this is also the put-in point for canoeists traveling up the Bog River Flow, the parking area tends to fill quickly.

One of the few marked trails in this region is the snowmobile trail leading from the Lower Dam to Trout Pond, a long, thin lake that is deep enough to harbor lake trout. Cross over the dam and enjoy the spectacle of the artificial waterfall. The old power house, which generated electricity for the Low Estate, stands nearby.

Following an old jeep road, irregularly marked with orange snowmobile discs, the trail gradually ascends a hardwood ridge about 150 feet above the dam, before descending almost that much to Trout Pond. Just before the road reaches the pond, it passes a waterfall that cascades over a steep cliff off to the right of the trail. Cliffs face the western side of the pond, which is lined with tall hemlock and white pine. On the left side of the lake you will find an old foundation and chimney, remnants of the Low Estate.

10 From Low's Lower Dam to Low's Upper Dam at Hitchins Pond

Canoeing, camping, swimming
3 miles, 1 hour, map II

Beyond the gate, the road slopes down to the dam and you can put your canoe in on the right. Note that motorboats are not permitted on the Bog River between the dams. The channel is quite narrow and as you paddle away from the noise of the falling water, the wild character of the river overtakes you. Large rock walls topped with tall white pines line much of the way. Nestled in the dense woods on your right are campsites 1, 2, and 3, within 0.7 mile of the dam. Swinging right at 0.8 mile, you will leave the steep banks behind and enter a boggy lowland lined with tall pines, tamaracks, and swamp maples. Another 0.2 mile takes you to a bend to the left where you can see the causeway of the Adirondack Division Railroad rising above the grassy swampland, 0.4 mile ahead. Beyond, the rocky face of an unnamed hill rises above the complex at Low's Upper Dam, still out of sight.

After passing under the railroad bridge, turn left and follow the gradually winding channel another 0.9 mile to Hitchins Pond. If you have time, you may wish to take a side trip into the small, scenic bay on the right. At its far end is the spruce swamp described in section 8. To continue on, paddle into the bay ahead and turn left. Campsite 4 is on your right, near a point of land that separates this bay and the upper part of the pond you enter next. Halfway through this section, you can find campsite 5 on the right shore.

As you approach the upper end of Hitchins Pond, civilization encroaches in a major way. Wooden and concrete abutments mark the remains of a boat dock, beyond which an engineered channel carries water from the base of the upper dam. A six hundred-foot gravel driveway leads away from the large clearing at the water's edge, passes a commodious three-story lodge where Low sometimes stayed, and ends at an intersection near the top of the upper dam. The road to the right, north, with the gate across it comes in from Horseshoe Lake (section 8), 2.6 miles away. The road to the left is an extension of County Route 10, coming in from Sabattis Station, 3 miles away. It is closed to the public, emerging from private land 0.8 mile from the dam. After crossing the dam, it swings around and continues up along the north side of the flow, entering the property of the Hiawatha Boy Scout Council, 2 miles away. People involved with the Scout camp and owners of a camp beyond regularly come in from Sabattis, so the road is maintained year-round.

There are more buildings at this intersection, and others in the woods to the right. In all, there are over a dozen structures, all severely vandalized. They are what remains of the Suffolk County Boy Scout Council's complex of shops, garages, and bunkhouses, most of which were originally part of Low's development. No camping is allowed in this area and because of its deplorable sight and potential safety hazards, you wouldn't want to. One redeeming curiosity exists here that is worth your attention. A small loop off the driveway near the boat dock has some intricate rockwork in it. Concrete pads hold the iron posts that once supported a flagpole. Embedded flat into the pads at carefully spaced intervals are six metal plates, each memorializing a deceased canine friend. Names such as "Low's Queen of Sheba," "Wizzer Hitchins," and "Black As Sin Of Hitchins" conjure up images of a special time when people, and animals, shared in the history of this place. There used to be a seventh plate; vandals have removed it.

11 Cliffs above Hitchins Pond

Easy but steep bushwhack, views
0.3 mile, 20 minutes, 360-foot vertical rise, map II

A steep ridge rises up behind Hitchins Pond, its fire-scarred top visible from Low's Upper Dam and the flow between the dams. The woods at its base is fairly open and a bearing of 345° magnetic from the intersection of roads will take you to the top. Starting right at the southern gate, you should, however, notice a herd path at the side of a ravine. If you are bushwhacking, you notice that as the tree cover diminishes, you must use judgment and caution negotiating the rock slabs. Their angles are tricky and scanning ahead will prevent you from coming to an impassable face. Toward the top, the exposed rock cliffs have yellow markers and haphazard rock cairns. You can follow them to each end of the ridge, but they fade out as you reenter the woods. Along the way, as you approach the high point near the west end, you will see a plaque bolted onto the rock that says "A. AUGUSTUS LOW/ AUGUST 1, 1889/ NOVEMBER 24, 1963."

You can walk for about 500 feet along the bare rock crest enjoying an exceptional view of great distance and unique perspective. Though intervening hills obscure the main body of Lows Lake, the long channel leading up to it is visible to the west and beyond it, hills in the southern Five Ponds Wilderness stretch for miles. The best view, however, is to the east. The lower flow winds away from Hitchins Pond through an extensive grassy swampland interrupted by stands of conifers and the Adirondack Division Railroad, which cuts across in a straight line. The southern edge of Horseshoe Lake is visible beyond, with Mount Morris farther behind. The High Peaks of the Seward Range and a distant Mount Marcy define the far horizon to the right, while to the left, Whiteface and McKenzie Mountains stand at the limit of your view.

The exposed rock owes its origin to the disastrous fires early in this century and the erosion that followed. As a result, the ridge is constantly under stress and the 1988 drought killed a number of trees and shrubs.

12 Lows Lake

Canoeing, camping, hiking, swimming, important bog areas and wildlife habitat
Over 9 miles of canoeing one way, maps II, III, and XIII

You can spend many days exploring Lows Lake and the Bog River Flow. Twenty-one designated campsites along most of its length, as well as several undeveloped sites, provide ample space for the solitary canoeist or large groups. The designated campsites are of varying size and distance from the water and most are marked with small numbered wooden squares which may be hard to see from a distance. Some may have improvised tables and fireplaces and at least one, #8, has an outhouse. Three other campsites on the south shore, designated Boone's Landing, Moose Bay Landing, and Virgin Timber Landing, are available by permit only during the months of June, July, and August. No camping is allowed on the three islands named Frying Pan, Gooseneck, and Pole during the same months. These two restrictions are based on a shared use agreement with the Hiawatha Boy Scout Council, which maintains a camp on the north shore. Old roads of varying condition offer opportunities for short walks or deep woods exploration. From the open ledges of two prominent ridges, far-reaching views extend beyond the flow to distant hills and ranges. As with all large bodies of water, the flow can be easily agitated by modest winds and paddlers should be cautious under such circumstances. There is no ordinance against motorboats above the upper dam, but they are rarely seen there. Existing topographic maps do not show the shoreline of Low's Lake accurately. The outlet of Bog Lake to the south is more grown in than shown, as is Tomar Pond and the extreme western bay, making it a little difficult to find the canoe carry to Big Deer Pond.

After canoeing between the dams (section 10), you will find that the carry up the driveway and over the dam to begin a canoe trek on the upper flow is short, just over 0.1 mile. The first 3 miles of canoeing above the upper dam are through an interesting channel that alternately widens and narrows. The south bank is an esker that extends west, with a few breaks, for over 4 miles. Campsites 6 through 9 lie along the 2 miles of state land shoreline on the north bank. They are not accessible from the road except by precise bushwhacks. A small floating bog lies across the flow 0.9 mile up from the dam. It holds a number of small tamaracks on a mat of sphagnum, sedges, and low heath shrubs. As of early 1989, a shallow channel on the north edge allows the best passage with minimum dragging and impact on the mat.

State land resumes on the south shore after 3 miles, and the flow swings around a pine-forested point on the right, beyond which the Scout camp has developed a beach and boat launch. The next mile of paddling swings you west again and takes you through the final narrows with tall pines on the right. This is the gateway to Lows Lake proper and if winds are high, it is advisable to stay near the north shore. Ahead are several islands and their western edges are high, eroded sand banks, typical of the weathered banks of such glacial terrain. The south shore here has numerous bays and side channels and if you are confused on the way out, steer between the large islands, with Frying Pan Island on your left.

The north shore becomes state land again soon after the islands and continues unbroken except for a small private parcel near the entrance to Grass Pond. A camp identifies the location of the private parcel. Campsites 10, 11, and 12 are in bays on the north shore while sites 13 through 17 line Grass Pond, the stump-filled entrance of which can be found behind an island after swinging north past the private camp.

If you are camping in the area, you might enjoy a chance to stretch your legs after the long paddle. The private road west from the gate at the upper dam emerges from the Boy Scout property at a gate and continues west to a fork, about 6.7 miles from the upper dam. The left fork goes south onto a peninsula, then west to the private camp. The right fork goes on to encircle Grass Pond, but it is no longer maintained, so it is becoming rough. Blowdown blocks it in a few places. But this stretch through recently acquired lands is a good trail for walking. A left turn, at a second fork 0.5 mile farther, leads straight west to campsite 13 and a former crossing of the Grass Pond outlet. This section of road is easily accessible from the bays near the fork onto the peninsula and from paths leading back from campsites 14 and 15. It touches all of the other campsites in the area but 10 and 12.

Many people feel that Grass Pond is one of the most scenic locations in the entire Bog River basin. This is hard to dispute when you paddle into the main body and look at the rugged crags on Grass Pond Mountain's western flank. Campsites benefit from the relative shelter of the pond, and traces of old logging roads leaving the main one invite the wilderness bushwhacker.

Another small bog floats near the north shore at the entrance to the dense west bay. The carry to Big Deer Pond and Oswegatchie River (section 14) starts at an unofficial campsite on a point in the southwest corner of this bay. Virgin Timber Landing is on a point near the southern approach to the bay and campsite 18 is farther in to the west.

Directly in the center of Lows Lake is a very large floating bog, seemingly anchored to an island on its southern edge. South of it, a smaller version of this bog-island arrangement hides the outlet of Bog Lake to the south. You can find Moose Bay Landing along the west bank of the outlet, which you can enter from either side of the bog. Just over 1 mile up the outlet is the causeway of an old road that came from Sabattis Station in the east and continued on toward Tomar Mountain. You can only hike it for less than a mile in either direction before coming to private land, but it passes through interesting grassy fields on the west and crosses a scenic vly on the east. Dense plantations of red and Scotch pine provide good cover for the snowshoe hare and ruffed grouse you may surprise. Campsite 19 is at the west end of the causeway, at the edge of a large open area. Two large culverts carry the water under the old roadway, but they are obstructed and not navigable. You can carry over the road or try your luck paddling through a washout to the right. The main channel is ahead to the right and 0.5 mile up it you will come to a boundary line in a marshy stretch posted by Robinwood Park, a sporting club which leases the property from the International Paper Company. State policy seems to indicate that you can legally proceed from here into Bog Lake as long as you do not set foot on the surrounding land, but Robinwood Park disputes that. It is another complex issue of riparian rights and until an official agreement is recognized, you will risk charges of trespass if you continue.

Proceeding east from the Bog Lake outlet, you will pass Boone's Landing and campsites 20 and 21 on the south shore. With so many interesting possibilities, a weekend trip into Lows Lake will be a hurried affair. A well-planned, extended stay will allow you to pace your explorations and fully enjoy the many features of this newer acquisition.

13   Grass Pond Mountain

Extensive views
0.3 mile by bushwhack, 0.5 mile by path, 35 minutes, 500-foot vertical rise, maps III and XIII

The cliffs on Grass Pond Mountain provide a spectacular view of Lows Lake and the surrounding country. Think of it as a slightly larger version of the ridge above Hitchins Pond (section 11) since the terrain is similar and the rewards are great. The approach begins on the north shore road, accessible by foot from several campsites as described in section 12. If you are canoeing over from other points, paddle into the tiny cove north of campsite 12 that is fed by a brook passing through a culvert under the road on the north edge. Beach your canoe here and walk west on the road as it rises slightly. A faint path that may be flagged by hunters heads north from a small turnout on the right. It dips to a wet crossing of a small marsh, then climbs north and east to the eastern end of a ridge leading west to the best lookouts. The markings along this route are unpredictable and there are a few slippery, eroded spots.

Many people choose to take a shorter but steeper route and bushwhack straight up the cliffs. Again, scan ahead and use caution and judgment in negotiating the rock for a safe, adventurous climb. The most direct course begins at the intersection in the road where the left fork goes to the private camp. This is about 400 feet west of the culvert. Head toward magnetic north to the base of the cliffs and begin climbing. If this looks too steep for you, walk to the left until the ascent angle suits your ability. As you climb, stay on bare rock as much as possible to avoid unnecessary damage of the mosses, lichens, and grasses clinging to the slope. Birch and mountain ash grow in stunted postures on this weathered face and blueberry shrubs lie low against the rock.

Lows Lake from Grass Pond Mountain

There is so much to see in the changing perspectives as you walk along the 500 feet of exposed cliff top. It is as if your map has come to life and you can now truly appreciate the nature of the area. From the western end, you can look down onto the deep blue surface of Grass Pond, surrounded by richly forested hills. Several floating bog mats are visible on the surface of the western end of the flow near the island in the Grass Pond outlet. The gentle contours of many unnamed hills and mountains in the Five Ponds Wilderness lie beyond. To the south, Mount Electra stands in the distance over the left edge of Tomar Pond, whose waters are slowly shrinking under the advance of bog and marsh vegetation. The two floating bogs near the outlet of Bog Lake stretch out before you, their attentive islands giving them anchoring for now. West Mountain, Wakely Mountain, Blue Ridge, and Blue Mountain are some of the more familiar shapes on the horizon. Working your way to the east, you are soon able to see the far end of Lows Lake where the flow disappears into the low valley. The bright, west-facing sand banks of the islands contrast with the water and pines they separate. The massive High Peaks of the Seward and Santanoni ranges frame the more distant summits of the MacIntyre Range and Mount Marcy.

This is not the true summit of Grass Pond Mountain. It is to the north and there are other cliffs between you and it. The added elevation is not significant and you cannot easily see Lows Lake from these cliffs, so plan to spend your entire afternoon enjoying the beauty of the area right where you are.

When Bob Marshall was at Summer Camp on Cranberry Lake (see the chapter on the Five Ponds Wilderness Area), he and fellow classmates cut out and marked a trail to Grass Pond Mountain. They reached the foot of the mountain via a route along logging roads that is now overgrown but suggests a great bushwhack north from Grass Pond to Darning Needle Pond (section 84) in the wilderness area. The route traverses a swamp where, even with the roads, hunters were known to become lost.

14 Big Deer Pond Canoe Carry

Trail, hiking, canoe carry
1 mile, 25 minutes, one easy grade, maps III, XIII, and XIV

Colvin, in his 1873 visit, named Big Deer Pond "Lost Lake." The carry to Big Deer Pond follows in part an old logging road that once traversed the Broadhead Gore. It begins in the extreme western bay of Lows Lake, at a spot on the southwest shore. It is wide, but rough in places and use of a wheeled carrier would be difficult. It is marked with yellow canoe-carry markers.

A sign marks the beginning of the carry where there is a large designated campsite, with another, smaller one to the left. The carry heads southwest and obliquely intersects an old logging road in 0.2 mile. Back to the left, the road trails off to the south of Lows Lake, becoming obscure in the vicinity of campsite 18. Ahead, to the right, the carry becomes smoother as it follows the old road over a gradual rise. The carry officially ends at a small campsite on the north shore of Big Deer Pond where a log dock provides an easy put-in. An unmarked path continues past the campsite and connects with the eastern network of trails in the Five Ponds Wilderness (section 81).

To reach the start of the canoe carry to the upper Oswegatchie River (section 83), paddle to the southwest shore of Big Deer Pond where a sign marks the take-out.

Nehasane Preserve

THE HERMIT DAVID Smith came to the Beaver River in 1820 hoping to find the solitude he craved. As loggers and "sports" began to work their way into the region, however, he was continuously forced to move farther upstream. He finally found peace at a large lake near the headwaters which came to be known as Smith's Lake. Some years later, Smith mysteriously disappeared, but his name remained a little longer.

In the 1880s and 1890s, huge tracts of land in the upper Beaver River area were bought by the railroad company executive Dr. William Seward Webb. He was a shrewd land speculator as well as a clever entrepreneur with the vision of building a rail line through the Adirondacks as an important business and transportation link between New York and Canada. He knew the role such a line would play in opening up the Adirondacks for development and tourism. He was also very successful, managing to complete construction of the line in 1892, within two years, despite obstacles presented by terrain, purchases of questionable land titles, and a hard-worked labor force. Webb's Adirondack Division of the New York Central Railroad, or the Mohawk and Malone Railroad as it was called, not only gave him access to his lands, but enhanced the value of those lands.

Webb's land holdings extended south from the Beaver River basin to the North Branch of the Moose River and are said to have encompassed 250,000 acres. Most of the land was timbered and eventually over half was sold, leaving 115,000 acres that Webb developed into Nehasane Park, his private Adirondack estate. The name supposedly is an Indian term meaning "beaver crossing river on a log," but this is hard to substantiate. Quite taken with the beauty of Smith's Lake, he renamed it Lake Lila after his wife, Lila Osgood Vanderbilt, and on its western shore he built the elegant Nehasane Lodge. Nehasane Station was his private station on the railroad. A siding held the private cars of the many affluent guests who visited the lodge.

After the 75,000-acre sale of land to the state of New York in the Stillwater Reservoir area, Webb was left with 40,000 acres in his park, 8,000 of which was enclosed by a nine-foot wire fence. Inside, he experimented with stocking black-tailed deer, elk, and moose until a portion of the fence was destroyed in the 1903 fires.

Forestry projects and lumbering operations were conducted throughout Nehasane Park and a select group of wardens and scientific foresters was hired to patrol it. When Dr. Webb died in 1926, the estate passed to his heirs, who formed their own enclaves within his park. In 1978, through the efforts of the Adirondack Conservancy, 14,600 acres were conveyed to the state. This parcel, commonly referred to as Nehasane Preserve, contains the 1409-acre Lake Lila and a long extension of land connecting it to the Five Ponds Wilderness to the west. Agreements were also reached which established various conservation, development, and access easements on the remaining lands, which were retained by the heirs.

Nehasane Lodge, which had fallen victim to neglect and vandalism, was demolished and removed by the state in 1984. It was a controversial action that caused great debate between historic preservationists who wanted the building refurbished, members of sporting clubs who wanted to repair and lease it, and environmentalists who wanted the land returned to its former, undeveloped state. Legalities concerning the presence and management of nonconforming structures on Forest Preserve land finally decided the fate of Dr. Webb's great camp.

15 Lake Lila

Canoeing, camping, fishing, lean-to, hiking
0.3-mile carry, map IV

Much of Lake Lila's shoreline is lined with tall, windswept pines, giving it a remote, primitive beauty. The rocky hills to the north, however, show the scars of past fires where vegetation has been slow to recover. Ravens and red-tailed hawks can be seen soaring high above the hills and osprey have been known to nest in the area in recent years. Great blue herons feed in the marshes and the sandbars are covered with the tracks of raccoons, fishers, and otters. Several pairs of common loons nest in the lake each year as do a variety of ducks.

To reach the Lake Lila Primitive Area from the south, drive north on NY 30 from its intersection with NY 28N in Long Lake. In 7 miles, you will see a sign to Sabattis at the intersection of County Route 10A. Turn left and drive 3 miles to the intersection of County Route 10, commonly referred to as the Sabattis Road, which turns left along the north side of

Little Tupper Lake. If you are coming from the north, drive south on NY 30 from its intersection with NY 3 in Tupper Lake. In 11.6 miles, the north end of County Route 10A turns right, near a sign to Sabattis. Follow it 3.1 miles to the intersection of the Sabattis Road at Little Tupper Lake. Head west on the Sabattis Road for 4.6 miles to the Lake Lila Access Road, which turns left. Follow this dirt road southwest for 5.8 miles until you come to a large parking area, just past the point where state land begins. The road continues past the parking area, but it is blocked by a barrier and the public is prohibited from driving farther. It is used by owners of adjacent private lands and the DEC for management purposes, but hikers can walk the road to the former lodge site and to reach Frederica Mountain (section 16). The access road is maintained year-round, but as of 1989, only foot travel was permitted along it in winter. In this case, as well as if the parking area is full, you must park well off on the side of the Sabattis Road and walk the entire 5.8 miles to the lake. Owners' restrictions and ongoing logging operations prohibit parking along the access road. To the left of the barrier is a register and on the south edge of the parking area is the beginning of the carry to the lake. It leads 0.3 mile to the upper end of the lake's long northeast bay and has been greatly improved in recent years by the addition of plank walkways over the muddy sections.

Lake Lila is currently the largest lake in the Adirondack Park entirely surrounded by Forest Preserve land. It offers excellent canoeing opportunities for day trips or multi-day excursions. There are fifteen designated campsites, four of them on islands, the rest along the shoreline. These are primitive tent sites of varying size, some with makeshift tables, and all are marked with yellow camping disks. The large clearing where the lodge stood is designated for group camping and is the only location with outhouses. A small lean-to is also available near the shore, just north of the clearing. Other locations may be used for camping as long as the 150-foot rule is observed. No camping is allowed within one quarter mile of the parking area. Only canoes and car-top boats may be used on the lake; no trailered or motorized craft are allowed.

Beside canoeing around the lake and exploring its islands, it is possible to canoe down the outlet for a mile before the river enters private lands. Posted signs and an old submerged log and chain boom alert you to this boundary and though many argue that you can legally proceed farther, carries around rapids and obstacles downstream necessitate trespassing. This is the official start of the Beaver River, and the trip through Nehasane Lake to Stillwater Reservoir would make a grand canoe route, but to date, the surrounding landowners stoutly refuse to negotiate a public easement.

The lake's main inlet, Shingle Shanty Brook, enters the southeast bay in the middle of a wide, grassy marsh. It is a sizeable tributary that drains at least a dozen ponds and lakes, and you can canoe it for at least 1.5 miles as it winds relentlessly through tall grasses and alders. You reach a private boundary just after a major change in direction points you south toward the alder-choked waters upstream; here you must turn around. Allow about an hour and a half for the round-trip navigation.

16 Frederica Mountain
Trail, hiking, views, access to campsites
4.8 miles, 2½ hours, 460-foot vertical rise, map IV

The road beyond the barrier at the parking area is designated as a hiking trail and has blue markers. Following gentle grades, you get your first view of the lake in a little over a half hour, at 1.6 miles, when the road nears the shore. A path here goes left for 100 feet to a wide sandy beach where a medium-sized campsite is located. It is a nice location for the non-canoeist who wishes to enjoy the region. After crossing Harrington Brook ten minutes later, you begin a gradual swing south-southeast. Twenty minutes later, 3 miles from the parking area, a path turns left and goes 90 feet to a small lean-to at the waters' edge. The view across the lake is exceptional on a clear day with the high peaks of the MacIntyre Range in the extreme distance. In this same area, an old road forks back to the right and climbs 0.1 mile up the hill to the railroad and Nehasane Station, which is still standing. This was the road over which Dr. Webb's guests rode in a fancy coach from the station to the lodge. If you choose to make the side trip up to explore the station, use care, since the building has been vandalized and is unsafe.

On the blue trail, you cross another brook beyond the intersection, after which you reach a clearing on the left, which is a designated group campsite. The road splits past the clearing at the 3.3-mile point. The left fork goes to the lodge site and more group camping areas, then proceeds for another mile where it enters private land. Signs direct you to turn right to continue on to Frederica Mountain and you will cross the railroad tracks in less than ten minutes. After passing an old beaver pond on the right, the road begins a steady ascent, leveling off in ten minutes. Just ahead on the right is a signpost marking the beginning of the foot trail up the mountain.

Map IV: Sections 15–17, 62, 83
Based on NY State DOT 7½ Nehasane Lake,
Brandreth Lake, Sabattis and USGS 7½ Wolf
Mountain Quadrangles.

- - - Trail
──── Road
•••••• Bushwhack
Ⓟ Parking
──── Canoe Route

Lake Lila from Frederica Mountain

The trail climbs steadily but easily through a handsome hardwood forest and you should reach the wooded summit in less than twenty minutes. Continue over the summit to the open rock ledges on the southeast face of the mountain. Most of the lake is visible below you, displaying its many bays and islands. In the east, you can trace the drainage of Shingle Shanty Brook and see a large tamarack swamp beyond. On the distant horizon, the Fishing Brook Range rises up to the left of flat-topped Blue Mountain. The massive Santanoni and Seward Ranges extend to the north; and, in the distance, the MacIntyre Range can be seen between them. Lesser mountains and hills stretch away to the south with Blue Ridge, Wakely Mountain, and West Mountain standing out as some of the more recognizable ones.

17 Mount Electra and Negro Lake

Hike and bushwhack to former fire tower summit and remote lake, map IV

Few fire towers are still in use in the Forest Preserve due to maintenance and manpower budget cuts and to the alternate method of aerial fire observation. Eventually, the abandoned towers fall victim to neglect and vandalism and many have been removed. Many of those still standing are climbed, although they are generally unsafe. The tower on Mount Electra has not been manned for several years; and, because it is in an advanced state of deterioration, it is hazardous to climb and any attempt to do so is not recommended. The trail to the summit has vanished and the tower is scheduled for removal. Without it, there will be no view from the densely wooded mountaintop.

A low valley at the eastern base of Mount Electra is flooded and the tall stands of dead timber present a scene of primeval desolation. If you hike south for 3 miles along the railroad tracks from the trail to Frederica Mountain, you will come to Partlow, the site of a former station that was the terminus for Nehasane Park's logging operations. A spur line ran north from here, through the valley to Sylvan Lake, later renamed Partlow Mildam. Its tracks are long gone, but the bed is still visible and depending on the intensity of flooding, you can follow it north for two miles before it enters private property. Some current topographic maps show an old road heading west to private land around Rock Lake. This road has all but disappeared as has the road north from Rock Lake to Negro Lake (see section 21 for a brief discussion of its name). The former 0.8-mile trail up Mount Electra began about 0.6 mile north, up the spur from Partlow.

About 1 mile north along the roadbed, the valley narrows, then opens up again to a smaller, but more severely flooded area. This is a very hard section to negotiate since it is also filled with blowdown. Several sandpits can be found at the north edge of the flooding and an obvious road heads west from them to climb along the northern shoulder of Mount Electra. After 1.3 miles it turns sharply to the right, passing northeast of Wilder Pond, and links up with the route of the old road to Negro Lake. This road is not hard to follow, but because of the difficulties encountered in getting to it, this 6.8-mile approach to the Negro Lake area is of questionable desirability. An alternate approach from the west is given in section 21.

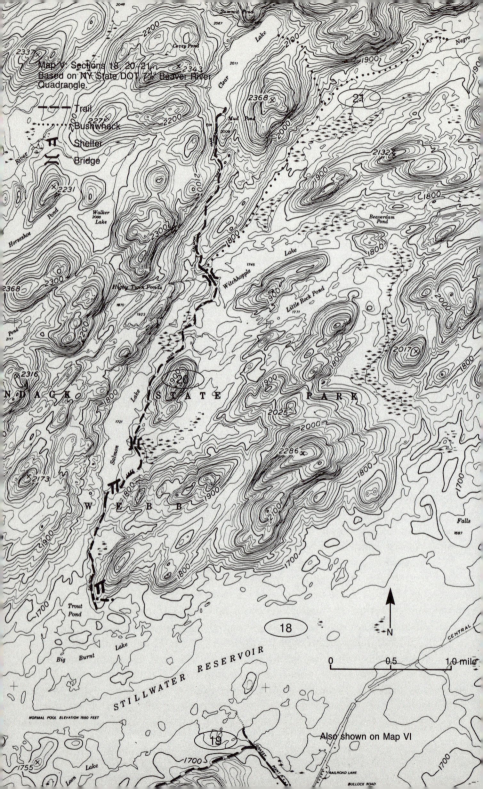

Map V: Sections 18, 20, 21.
Based on NY State DOT 7½' Beaver River
Quadrangle.

Trail
Bushwhack
Shelter
Bridge

ADIRONDACK STATE PARK

WEBB

STILLWATER RESERVOIR

NORMAL POOL ELEVATION 1680 FEET

Also shown on Map VI

N

0   0.5   1.0 mile

18

19

Stillwater Reservoir and the Beaver River

WITH THE DEMANDS that industries and the state canal system put on the Black River in the second half of the nineteenth century, the need for a regulated water supply became critical. Engineers surveyed its tributaries and headwaters intensely, hoping to solve the problem by constructing an elaborate system of reservoirs that could release their waters in a reliable flow pattern. The Beaver River, a major source of water for the lower Black River, was an obvious choice for control. A dam, completed in 1887 and raised to eighteen feet in 1893, was built at the foot of the Beaver River Flow or, as it was also known, the Stillwater. The dam was improved in 1922, when the reservoir attained its present size of 6700 acres.

It is interesting to note that when the state built the dam at Stillwater, some of the land it flooded was in Dr. William Seward Webb's Nehasane Park. He claimed the subsequent raising of the dam damaged his timber resource and made it impossible to harvest timber on 66,000 acres. In a shrewd and ethically controversial move, he filed a lawsuit against the state. Arguments fell in his favor and the state was forced to buy 75,000 acres for $600,000—the largest single acquisition the state has ever made for lands for the Forest Preserve. The cost was higher than the going rate for forest land and made quite a profit for Webb.

Today, the hamlet of Stillwater contains several homes and camps, a general store, a restaurant, and the headquarters of the local Forest Ranger. A public boat launch is located at the edge of the reservoir, where you will also find a map of the area, a pavilion, a few docks, and a generous parking area.

Access to Stillwater from the north and west is by turning east off NY 12 onto River Street in the village of Lowville. River Street becomes Number Four Road outside the village limits and reaches the settlement of Bushes Landing in 4.4 miles, where it forks left. In 13.6 more miles, at the settlement of Number Four, the road turns right, becoming the Stillwater Road. Pavement ends here and a left turn leads 0.4 mile to the reservoir.

To reach Stillwater from the south, turn north off NY 28 in the center of Eagle Bay and follow Big Moose Road 17 miles to its intersection with the

Stillwater Reservoir

Number Four Road. Turn right and proceed to the reservoir, 0.4 mile away. Much of the road on each approach to Stillwater is dirt and subject to rapid snow accumulation, frost heaving, and washouts, the Big Moose Section being the worse.

18 Stillwater Reservoir

Canoeing, camping, fishing, swimming, maps V and VI

A register is located near the Ranger's Headquarters, to the right of the boat launch area. In addition to signing in, you are requested to state your campsite and move a marker from the available campsite board to the in-use board. There are forty-six designated campsites of various sizes, some with makeshift tables and benches. They are primitive tent sites and are marked with small numbered wooden squares that may be hard to see at a distance. Three are designated group sites for ten to twenty people. Other locations on Forest Preserve land are acceptable as long as the 150-foot limit is observed. Motorboats are regularly in use, but are restricted by natural hazards such as stumps, boulders, sandbars, and shoals. When the water is low, the broad, sandy beaches change the landscape and make it difficult to spot landmarks along the shore. Because of its size, the reservoir is subject to rough periods during moderate winds, making canoeing difficult and even dangerous.

19 Old Beaver River Road

Canoe or ski 1 mile to start, hiking, skiing
5.5 miles, 2½ hours, map VI

When the reservoir was raised to its present level, the western 1.3 miles of the 6.8-mile road from Stillwater to the hamlet of Beaver River was flooded over. This effectively isolated Beaver River, giving rise to its remote "frontier town" image. It is not so removed as you might think, however; you can still reach it by boat, canoe, floatplane, snowmobile, and trail. A local barge still transports vehicles to the area and homebuilt vehicles ride in on the tracks of the Adirondack Division Railroad. The derelict Beaver River Station still stands and there is an old hotel, the Norridgewock, as well as a remodeled restaurant and bar to liven this living museum.

You can reach the old road by canoe or by crossing the frozen water on skis or snowshoes. Head due east for about a mile from the boat launch area to the opposite shore where you will see the opening in the trees. A boat ramp marks the beginning of the road, which is also known as Flow Road or Six-mile Road. It makes an easy but uneventful trip. It is heavily used by snowmobiles in winter and Beaver River residents drive on it in summer (with no place else for their vehicles to go, none have license plates). At 3.1 miles, you reach the south shore of Loon Lake, a large body of water that is actually connected to the reservoir by a narrow channel; 1.7 miles more takes you to the intersection with Grass Point Road. If you head north on it for 0.2 mile, you reach a boat ramp on the reservoir, while heading south, you reach the community of Beaver River in 0.7 mile.

20 Salmon, Witchhopple, and Clear Lakes

Trail accessible by canoe, hiking, lean-tos, camping, swimming, fishing, hunting
5.5 miles canoeing, 4.5 miles total on foot, 5½ hours, 340-foot vertical rise, maps V and VI

The north shore of Stillwater Reservoir is part of the Five Ponds Wilderness Area. The only official DEC foot trail along that shore leads to a cluster of ponds in the Wilderness Area. To reach the trailhead, paddle straight up the flow from the boat launch area to a point where the

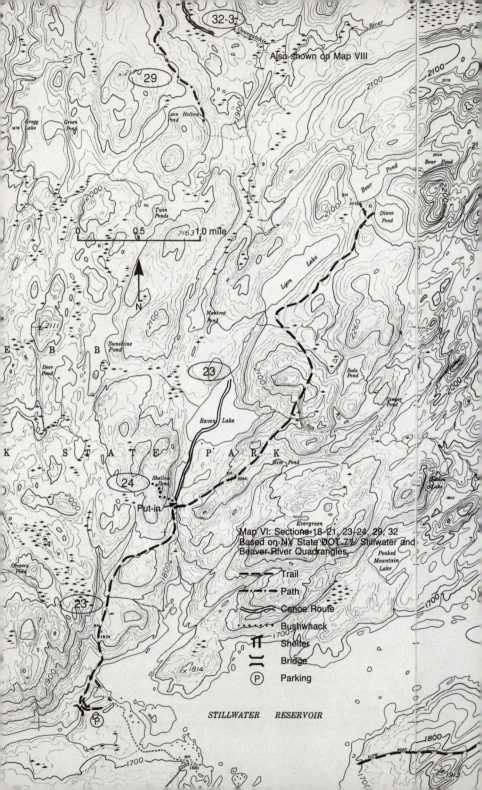

Also shown on Map VIII

32-3

29

Gregg Lake

Green Pond

Loon Hollow Pond

River

Bear Pond

Diana Pond

Lyon Lake

Twin Ponds

0.5   2163 1.0 mile

N

Muskrat Pond

Soda Pond

2260

Sunshine Pond

Ginger Pond

23

Deer Pond

Raven Lake

PARK

Hidden Lake

Sim Pond

24

Shallow Pond

Put-in

Evergreen

Map VI: Sections 18-21, 23-24, 29, 32
Based on NY State DOT 7½' Stillwater and
Beaver River Quadrangles.

Peaked Mountain Lake

Crapsey Pond

Trail
Path
Canoe Route
Bushwhack
Shelter
Bridge
Parking

23

P

STILLWATER   RESERVOIR

Also shown on Map V

reservoir narrows, just over 4 miles away. Bear left into the channel that leads to a large bay known as Big Burnt Lake. Just inside the channel, a smaller channel comes in on your left. Follow it north and east into a smaller bay called Trout Pond. The trail begins at the north edge of the pond where a large stream flows into it. You can also reach the trail from a good 0.5-mile long path that starts at the cove beyond campsite 19 on Big Burnt Lake.

Salmon, Witchhopple, and Clear Lakes are sometimes called the Red Horse Chain. One story explaining the name reflects the fact that in spring, raging, tannin-colored waters of their outlet stream resemble stampeding chestnut horses. The route to the ponds is also referred to as the Red Horse Trail, and as wilderness trails go, it is one of the best.

As a matter of fact, one of the first projects of the Adirondack Mountain Club was the establishment of a through trail from Wanakena to Grassy Point on the Beaver River Flow. The Red Horse portion was completed by the Conservation Department; the marking was done by Richard M. Jesup, a vice-president of the club in its first year, 1922, and a grandnephew of Morris K. Jesup, one of the moving spirits in the establishment of the Forest Preserve in 1885. Expansion of Stillwater Reservoir contributed to the discontinuance of the "old ADK yellow trail" as a through route.

Today, the Red Horse Trail heads north, paralleling the outlet of Salmon Lake and passing through a beautiful mature mixed woods. A diverse understory of ferns, clubmosses, and wildflowers lines the trail; easy grades allow you to enjoy your surroundings with little effort.

Following blue DEC markers north, you will come to a very good lean-to and outhouse 100 feet up from Trout Pond. Paralleling the stream to your left, you cross a little feeder on a small wooden bridge, then enter an area of large white cedars and tall white pines. Fifteen minutes later you arrive at Salmon Lake, 0.8 mile from Trout Pond. Another nice lean-to and outhouse are located here.

The trail swings east, away from the lake, then turns north, passing a wet vly on the right. You cross the stream that drains it on a plank bridge, about fifteen minutes from the lean-to. Afterward, you seldom see the lake as you continue on to another stream crossing thirty minutes later. Witchhopple Lake, twenty minutes beyond, and small open areas near the trail make good spots to camp or drop your pack and rest. Directly across the lake, in the distance you can see Mount Electra. The hike from Trout Pond to Witchhopple is just under 3 miles.

Continuing north over a small rise on the trail, you come to an open

Salmon Lake

area where you cross the outlet of Witchhopple Lake on a narrow plank bridge. Reentering the woods, you cross and recross the outlet of Clear Lake on planks. The trail begins a steady ascent and becomes a bit rougher as it swings away from the outlet and the increase in elevation takes you into a tall hardwood-dominated forest. In under an hour from Witchhopple, the trail levels off and you will see a small swampy widening of the Clear Lake outlet to the right. This is known as Mud Pond, and you will encounter dense evergreens and a few wet spots in this area. Clear Lake is just ahead, however, and from a small campsite near its outlet, you can rest, have lunch and enjoy the view up the lake to the rocky flanks of Summit Mountain. There are two rowboats in the area which you may want to use to explore the lake or fish.

Old maps and early accounts from the area document the fact that the trail once went farther, passing Crooked Lake and the upper reaches of the Robinson River on its way to High Falls on the Oswegatchie River. This six-mile section is now obscure, but for the experienced, well-equipped bushwhacker, trying to trace its probable course is an exciting challenge. Advanced navigational skills, meticulous planning, and a high degree of endurance are necessary however, since this rugged, seldom-traveled region is considered by many to be one of the wildest in the state.

21 ° Negro Lake
Moderate bushwhack, camping, fishing, maps V and VI

Negro Lake appears on different topographic maps as "Nigger Lake" or "Niger Lake," possibly relating to its tannin color. The governor has mandated that all place names with racial connotations be changed, so one can expect that this one will ultimately be renamed.

The lake is also considered to be part of the Red Horse Chain, since its outlet flows into the upper end of Witchhopple Lake. Following this outlet is one possible approach to Negro Lake, but wetlands along the way may require annoying detours to avoid wet feet or dense growth. Another possible approach is from the upper end of Clear Lake. A bushwhack southeast takes you through a saddle in a ridge and down to the outlet.

Once you reach Negro Lake, you will notice a natural dam at a narrows near its outlet. The dam may be part of a small esker or mound of glacial till. A road along the north side of the lake once crossed over to the south side of this dam and you can still trace its route. At the eastern end of this road, it meets another road coming south from private lands to the north. This road passes between the eastern end of the lake and a sandpit on the left, then heads south and east to the Partlow spur railroad bed described in section 17. On a point of land on the north shore, not far from the eastern end, a building once stood. It was razed and several of the trees that surrounded it were badly burned. The clearing has been used in the past as a campsite, but it can get quite windy.

22   Beaver River Impoundments
Canoeing, map VII

Niagara Mohawk maintains a series of dams downstream from Stillwater on the Beaver River. A 12-mile canoe route stretches west along the Beaver impoundments to a point outside the boundary of the Adirondack Park. It includes Taylorville Pond, Effley Falls Pond, Soft Maple Reservoir, and Beaver Lake, all of whose shorelines are privately owned. There are three access points along the Beaver chain, several designated carries, and one campsite open to the public.

The levels of the reservoirs change considerably as water is drawn for power. The portages are designed to avoid the dangerous areas near power stations and tend to be quite long.

Witchhopple Lake

The route begins at the Moshier Hydro Station, about 2 miles downstream from Stillwater on the Beaver. Turn north from Number Four Road onto Moshier Road and follow it for 0.6 mile to a parking area. The put-in is downstream from the power station. Canoe through Beaver Lake and along the river to the first portage, a 4000-foot carry along an access road that ends below the Eagle Hydro power station at Soft Maple Reservoir. About halfway along that reservoir, there is a marked campsite in a sandy bay where Niagara Mohawk Power Company permits the public to camp without charge.

A canal connects the two portions of Soft Maple Reservoir. At the western end of the reservoir, there is a 1000-foot carry down a steep hill to a launch point in Effley Pond. A dirt road parallels the south side of the Beaver. It is a 15-mile drive between the Moshier Road put-in and the put-in at Effley Falls Pond. That put-in can be reached by driving west from Belfort.

You canoe across Effley Falls Pond, take out and carry on the north side around Effley Dam for 800 feet downslope to Elmer Pond. The fourth portage, 400 feet, is around the Elmer power station to Taylorville Pond. The take-out is on the north shore of Taylorville Pond. You can reach the field where parking is permitted by driving east from Belfort on the Belfort-Long Pond Road for 1.3 miles.

Even with the portages, you can canoe this route in a long day, but driving between the put-ins to spot a car requires two or more hours.

Wilderness Lakes Tract and the Pepperbox Wilderness

IN 1982, THE State of New York acquired the 5929-acre Fisher Tract north of Stillwater Reservoir, then owned by Creative Forest Resources, a timber products company. The parcel is characterized by steep hills and several modest bodies of water which have led to its designation as the Wilderness Lakes Tract. According to the terms of the transaction, logging operations will continue until the end of 1990, after which all nonconforming structures must be removed and motorized vehicles will be prohibited. The tract will then be reclassified from Primitive to Wilderness. A dirt road that crosses the Beaver River just below the dam at Stillwater penetrates the area as it heads 5 miles northeast to private land around Bear Pond. It has been greatly improved to facilitate logging activities and is the principal access into the tract. When logging operations end, the road may be marginally maintained as far as the outlet of Shallow Pond to facilitate access to a 10-acre private inholding on the south shore of Raven Lake, and it would then be classified as a Primitive corridor. New and old logging roads branch off in several areas, providing further routes for exploration.

Exploring the tract to discover interesting destinations was thwarted by the dismal and depressing aspect of the current logging operations. Give it a few years to recover and then the roads will become wilderness paths to the dozen or so concealed lakes.

The significance of the Wilderness Lakes Tract acquisition, apart from the addition of more woodland acreage to the Forest Preserve, is its strategic location as a link between the southern end of the Five Ponds Wilderness to the east and the Pepperbox Wilderness to the west. One of the state's smaller wilderness areas, the 14,600-acre Pepperbox Wilderness is also one of its least known or used. Lying north of the Beaver River

Shallow Pond in the Wilderness Lakes Tract

below Stillwater Reservoir, it is one of the least "developed" parcels in the Park. Lumbering came relatively late to the region, but by the turn of the century, much of the timber was being cut and floated down Alder and Moshier creeks, the two main waterways that drain the area. In the 1920s, near a lumber camp on an interior pond, an old can of black pepper was found wired to a tree along the outlet creek. The name "Pepperbox" was given to the pond, the creek, and eventually to the surrounding land. Subsequent fires destroyed much of the remaining timber and after years of negotiations the state acquired the land in 1932. Despite the loss of its old-growth forest, the area has made a remarkable comeback and since there are no trails, lean-tos, or other facilities, the sense of wilderness here rivals, and frequently exceeds, that of the larger, more congested Forest Preserve parcels. With its diverse habitat, wildlife is abundant and you may see signs of mink, otter, fisher, bobcat, varying hare, and marten as well as the more familiar Adirondack mammals.

Low rolling hills, miles of streams, and numerous ponds and wetlands characterize the area, and by observing a few basic principles, you can spend days exploring these features. Though paths of hunters and anglers as well as the faint remains of old logging roads can occasionally be followed, you should be experienced in wilderness navigation and make frequent use of map and compass. In general, hills and ridges will likely be covered by poplar, beech, maple, black cherry, and hemlock, providing a fairly open terrain. Lowlands along swampy streambeds and lakeshores usually support dense spruce and balsam stands and can be extremely difficult to walk through. During the winter freeze, however, it is quite easy and enjoyable to follow the waterways from one area to the next. You can find campsites on some of the ponds, but they are often hard to locate since some were previously reached by floatplane before Wilderness classification ended that form of access.

Visitors to the Pepperbox in spring and summer are impressed by the blackflies and mosquitos, claiming they are worse here than anywhere else in the park. Winter visitors find snowshoes the easiest way to visit and travel between the marshy shored ponds and their interconnecting wetlands.

The following descriptions are offered as suggested routes to introduce you to the region and can be used as beginnings for adventures deeper into this true wilderness area.

Falls on Shallow Lake Outlet

23 Shallow Pond and Raven Lake

Canoeing
2-mile carry, 1 mile of canoeing, 2 hours, map VI

At first, this appears to be quite impractical, a long carry for a short canoe trip. However, when you consider the advantage of transporting your canoe over the road and the solitude you are likely to find, it is worth considering. This is a nice diversion from the reservoir and river traffic and can be just the beginning of a longer route for the wilderness paddler with a kayak or pack canoe.

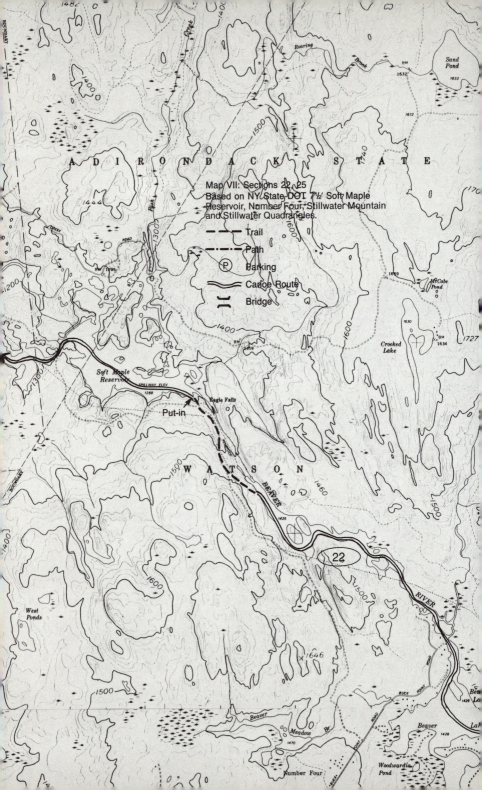

ADIRONDACK STATE

Map VII: Sections 22, 25
Based on NY State DOT 7½' Soft Maple
Reservoir, Number Four, Stillwater Mountain
and Stillwater Quadrangles.

— — — Trail
— · — · Path
ⓟ Parking
〰〰〰 Canoe Route
⊐⊏ Bridge

WATSON

Put-in

Eagle Falls

Soft Maple Reservoir

SPILLWAY ELEV
1289

Crooked Lake

McCabe Pond

Sand Pond

Roaring Brook

BEAVER

RIVER

22

West Ponds

Beaver Meadow Br.

Number Four

Woodwardia Pond

Buck Point

The road leading to the dam and Wilderness Lakes Tract forks left in Stillwater just before the Stillwater Restaurant. It heads north, passing west of the dam and reaches the Beaver River 1.3 miles from the intersection. There is a small place to park on the right and a register is on the right, just before the bridge over the river. On the other side of the river, the road swings right and you pass a large sandpit on the left. It is on state land, but will continue to be used as a source of material for road maintenance for the duration of logging operations. The land on your right is a restricted right-of-way around the dam for the Hudson River-Black River Regulating District.

The road begins a long, steady ascent, interrupted by occasional dips and flat stretches. The Pepperbox Wilderness is on your left and the Wilderness Lakes Tract Primitive Area is on the right. After 2 miles you will reach Shallow Pond on your left and this is where your canoe trip begins. Paddle north up the pond and through the channel that connects it with Raven Lake. A sizeable, attractive lodge is located on the south shore, to the right of the outlet on a 10-acre private parcel. Its owner appreciates the serenity of this lake as much as you will and its presence shouldn't detract from your enjoyment of the area.

24   Lookout above Shallow Pond and Falls on the Outlet

Easy bushwhacks, views
2.2 miles, 1¼ hours, 480-foot vertical rise, map VI

The eastern boundary of the Pepperbox Wilderness follows the dirt road for 2 miles, then goes north, leaving the road just before Shallow Pond. A small ridge rises to the west of the pond and from a small open area on its southern end, you can get a nice view over Shallow Pond, Raven Lake, and the western end of Stillwater Reservoir. To reach the open area, bushwhack north along the old yellow paint blazes of the boundary line or along the western edge of the pond for about 500 feet, then head west on an approximate bearing of 290° magnetic. This will take you almost 200 feet up the steep hillside onto the exposed rock of the lookout.

On the opposite side of the road, the outlet of Shallow Pond flows into a small pool, then drops about 12 feet through a rocky cut before continuing south to the reservoir. This pretty little waterfall is about 200 feet downstream from the road and is especially attractive in times of high water.

Shallow Pond and Raven Lake from the lookout above Shallow Pond

25 Southwestern Access to the Pepperbox Wilderness

0.3-mile access trail, map VII

Moshier Road turns north off Stillwater Road, 6.3 miles west of the reservoir. It leads to the Moshier Falls power plant on the Beaver River where the Niagara Mohawk canoe route begins. At 0.6 mile, there is a parking area and register on the right side of the road, while the access trail, which is also the canoe carry, starts on the opposite side. It is well marked with a large sign and bright green paint blazes, as well as blue DEC markers. After dropping down from the road, you head 400 feet north to a footbridge over Sunday Creek, a major tributary originating in the Independence River Wild Forest to the south. The canoe put-in is 100 feet farther on the right, below the power plant. The trail continues ahead from the put-in for another 100 feet to a bridge over the Beaver River. Beyond the river, you reenter the woods, then follow along the edge of a power line right-of-way, which you soon cross. On the opposite side, the trail officially ends at the beginning of the Wilderness Area, 0.3 mile from the road. Signs tell you that there are no marked foot trails beyond, but it is possible to follow hunters' paths along a stream to the west, which head north to a series of ponds 1.5 miles away. Other paths head east along the Beaver River, which is reduced in size in this area because of diversion by the power plant.

Watson's East Triangle

IN 1796, JAMES Watson purchased over 60,000 acres in two tracts that bordered John Brown's Tract on the north and west. His son's attempts to build a landed estate on Watson's West Triangle ended as almost all such attempts did—in failure. According to the historian Donaldson, on the son's death in 1839, the tracts were divided among forty-four cousins. The western triangle comprises part of the Independence River Wild Forest. Much of the eastern triangle remained in private hands.

In 1986, the state purchased a 16,288-acre tract, Watson's East Triangle, from International Paper Company. It not only provides some interesting recreational opportunities, but it is an important link in creating one of the largest contiguous pieces of state-owned wild lands in the Adirondacks. The acquisition agreement gave the hunting clubs who had leased the land rights to retain their hunting camps until September 1991.

The main logging haul road is currently open to the public and can be driven for 9 miles through what is now Forest Preserve, 10.8 miles from the gate. This road ends at a gate which blocks further vehicle access. Side roads from the main haul road, leading to ponds and hunting camps, are off limits to vehicle traffic, but are open for foot travel and winter skiing. They make pleasant excursions, as they usually lead to abandoned lumber camps or to charming interior ponds, often with one of the remaining hunting camps on its shores.

In addition to the numerous scenic ponds, Watson's East Triangle also comprises many miles of the Middle Branch of the Oswegatchie River and the headwaters of its West Branch. The spruce-fir forests along the rivers and the triangle's many creeks are extensive enough that they harbor many deer in winter, and are home to many boreal species, among them Canada jays—the lumberman's Whiskey Jack—and the pine marten.

Until the 1950s, Bergrens, which was located at the gate at the start of the haul road, was a lodging house and rustic sportsmen's hotel. The meals served here by the German-born proprietors and the quality of the deer hunting drew people from distant places.

West Branch Oswegatchie on the trail to Jakes Pond

As with the adjoining Aldrich Pond Wild Forest, to which it is linked on the north by a series of logging roads, Watson's East Triangle was most important for its role in the lumber industry. Like logging camps everywhere, the camps in Watson's East were self-contained, dependent on subsistence agriculture for food and forage for work horses and on hunting for wild game. Vestiges of these camps live on on the old topo maps— Kelly's Camp, Scanlon's Camp, Camp #1. They also live on in an ever dwindling number of people who recall these halcyon days. Openings in the unbroken forest with their remnants of old foundations and apple trees still give witness to these settlements.

Three main flows were created by dams to facilitate the floating of logs to downstream sawmills. In order downriver were Moynehan Flow, Alder Bed Flow, and Maple Hill Flow, which was just outside Watson's East. These old flows exist today mainly as flatwater stretches meandering in wide marshes and alder-fringed floodplains.

The Moynehan brothers—Dennis and Patrick—are closely connected to the opening of the area by lumbermen at the turn of the century. They built the original road through the area. It began near what is now Stillwater Reservoir. The main haul road travels over portions of this route today. The Moynehan brothers are also noted for being partners along with members of the Whitney family in the founding of Whitney Park near Tupper Lake. This is still the largest private park in the Adirondacks today.

A sample of the recreational opportunities present in Watson's East Triangle follows. This list will undoubtedly change as a Unit Management Plan is written for the area.

ACCESS TO WATSON'S EAST TRIANGLE

From the south, take Belfort Road northeast from NY 812 at Croghan and cross the Beaver River on a bridge at Belfort; turn left as soon as you cross the bridge. From the north take Erie Canal Road east from NY 812, 11 miles south of the intersection of NY 3 and 812. In 4 miles, turn left to the crossroads of Belfort, where Long Pond Road continues straight ahead.

Head east on Long Pond Road, which veers left at 2.2 miles and continues for 10.3 miles to the gate at the edge of Watson's East Triangle. You quickly leave farming country and enter huge sugar bushes where maple sap is tapped using the most modern equipment. Just before the gate is the parking lot for the short spur trail to Jakes Pond. The Belfort-Long Pond Road continues as the main haul road of Watson's East Triangle.

26 Watson's East Main Haul Road
Cross-country skiing, vehicular access to interior trails and ponds
10.8 miles, map VIII

The main haul road is the principal access to Watson's East and vehicles may be driven with care along its 10.8-mile, winding, rocky route from gate to gate. Because it is not plowed in winter, it makes a great ski route, especially when snowmobiles have packed down a good base to ski on. The way is wide and bumpy, with several moderate hills along the way. Heavy lumbering along the road has produced a successional forest of red maple, black cherry, and white ash. Trees of the more mature forest—sugar maples, hemlock, and yellow birch—and of the species that pioneer after a fire—grey birch and aspen—are for the most part missing. Beech, which provides mast for wildlife, is abundant. Beech is not favored for either lumber or pulp and the remaining uncut stands are infected with beech scale disease. The forests here are a laboratory where you can observe the future composition of stands that have been so severely logged.

Snowmobile use of the road can be heavy, especially on weekends, so watch out for them. Begin skiing at the gate at Bergrens. For the first 1.6 miles the road passes through private lands where the easement granting access to the road restricts you to the road itself. At 1.6 miles, you reach Forest Preserve lands.

A road forks right at 1.8 miles and reaches Desert Creek in 0.5 mile. Desert Creek is a corridor of marsh grass framed by spruce-fir, typical of the area's wetlands.

The tote road to Wolf Pond (section 28), forks left at 4.7 miles. Beyond the fork, you climb one of the steepest hills in the region, locally known as Parquet Hill. At 7.2 miles there is a hunting camp on the left, and although they will soon be removed, you should respect these private buildings. At 7.7 miles, an indistinct tote road forks left. It leads to the Wolf Pond log road and, after 4 miles, the Middle Branch of the Os-wegatchie by a confusing maze of interconnected log roads.

The main road continues winding and undulating, passing more skid and log roads. Many of these lead to abandoned lumber camps. At approximately 9.8 miles, you reach High Landing; below, at the bottom of the gulf, you can see the river flowing between evergreen-lined banks. On the road just beyond is the closest approach to the river for a canoe put-in for section 32; alternatively, you can put in just beyond the second gate.

On the right, at 10.5 miles, is the spur road to Buck Pond; just beyond and also on the right at 10.6 miles is the spur road to Hog Pond and Tied Lake (section 27).

You reach the south gate at 10.8 miles, just at a point where Gregg Creek flows under the road on its way to the Middle Branch. If you have driven this far, further vehicle traffic is prohibited, but you can park to the left of the road and continue on the Old Moynehan Road on foot (section 29).

27 Hog Pond and Tied Lake

Path, esker, hiking, cross-country skiing
2.2 miles round trip, relatively level, map VIII

At 10.6 miles on the main haul road, 0.2 mile short of the southern gate, a side road leads right to private land and two of the area's more attractive glacial ponds. The owners of this inholding have permission to drive this road through state land, but it is not for the public. It is a short, refreshing walk or ski to the ponds.

In the first 0.5 mile after you leave the main haul road you climb a rather steep ridge. Hog Pond is visible, nestled below the ridge on the right. This ridge is actually an esker, the remnant of a Pleistocene river that flowed beneath the glacier. From it you have an excellent view of the pond—an elongate, deep sheet of water framed beneath towering hemlocks. Hemlock, with scattered white pine, also crown the esker.

Hog Pond's name derives from the semi-feral pigs kept here in the early part of the century by Leon Kelly, who had a nearby logging camp.

The esker the road is following divides the drainage of two rivers here. It separates Hog Pond's outlet—which, with Buck Pond, is generally considered the source of the West Branch of the Oswegatchie River—from Gregg Creek, which flows into the Middle Branch just beyond where it crosses the main haul road at south barrier gate.

Continue on the road to Tied Lake at 1 mile. It is a dark dimple in the forest, enveloped by a spruce swamp. One of the hunting camps that will remain until 1991 is on the lake. While the road goes on another 0.2 mile to a gate at private land, you should turn back here. The spur is all the more remarkable in that Alder Brook, the outlet of Tied Lake, flows into a third river, the Beaver.

Hog Pond

28 Wolf Pond and Beyond

Path
7 miles round trip, map VIII

This logging road, punctuated by beaver flooding and washed out bridges, takes you to another of the typical ponds in the Watson's East Triangle. In addition, with a lot of map work and a little luck, this log road begins a route that penetrates the maze of local logging roads and eventually reaches a point on the Middle Branch of the Oswegatchie, directly across from the Middle Branch Trail (see section 37). If you want to use that route to continue on to Streeter Lake and the Aldrich Pond Wild Forest, you have to make a very difficult crossing of the Middle Branch, something that is not really advisable.

The start of this walk is the log road forking left, 4.7 miles along the main haul road. Near the beginning, the path veers around Wolf Pond, which has extensive wetlands along its outlet, semi-drowned spruce-fir on its fringe, and one of the remaining hunting camps.

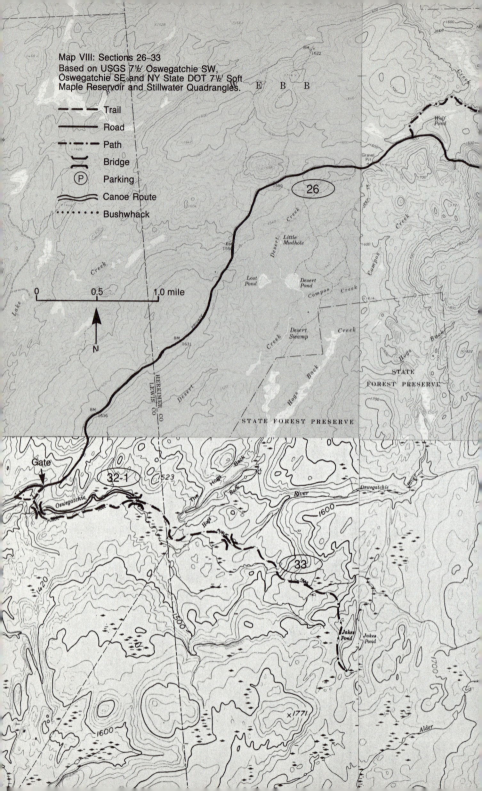

Map VIII: Sections 26–33
Based on USGS 7½' Oswegatchie SW,
Oswegatchie SE and NY State DOT 7½' Soft
Maple Reservoir and Stillwater Quadrangles.

- - - Trail
——— Road
-·-·- Path
Bridge
(P) Parking
Canoe Route
········ Bushwhack

0   0.5   1.0 mile

N

Also shown on Map XV

At 0.6 mile, you cross Wolf Pond outlet. The bridge is out but with care you can cross on the beaver dam. At 1 mile, a small tributary of Wolf Creek has also been flooded by beaver, but they have also graciously provided a dam here for the crossing. At 1.7 miles, the roadway crosses over the outlet of Massawepie Lake and continues to a T intersection at 3.5 miles. The way right leads back to the Main Haul Road in approximately 2 miles of confusing turns. The way left has even more confusing turns and until it is marked all the way to the Oswegatchie, you may be safer turning around and going back to the Main Haul Road.

29   Old Moynehan Road
Path, cross-country skiing, old-growth timber, canoeing
5.6 miles round trip, maps VI and VIII

The main haul road is gated at 10.8 miles, 9.2 miles after it enters Forest Preserve land. Several log roads branch from it to a string of wild, remote glacial ponds. The most noteworthy are described in sections 30 and 31.

Beyond the gate, the road leads to several private inholdings, but all further vehicular traffic is prohibited. The path here follows the route of the original logging road, constructed around the turn of the century by the Moynehan brothers. It is quite a suitable road for a summer walk or the continuation (albeit a long one) of the ski route on the haul road.

Walking south on the gravel roadway beyond the gate, you pass a side road to Brindle and Grassy ponds on the left at 0.2 mile. The haul road undulates through a mostly deciduous forest that was heavily cut over. At 0.6 mile, the logging road to Upper South Lake forks left. Shortly beyond, at 0.8 mile, you enter a parcel of land that was state-owned when the Forest Preserve was established. For the next 0.3 mile, the path goes through what is in essence a true old-growth or virgin stand. Notice the magnificent, straight yellow birch and red spruce, though many of the giants are on the ground, slowly decaying away—victims of the 1950 blowdown.

A bridge spans the Middle Branch of the Oswegatchie at 1.5 miles, and just beyond you can see a large, old beaver flow off to the right. This is Moynehan Flow. The gravel roadway continues 2.8 miles to a private inholding where further access is blocked by a gate.

High Landing on the Middle Branch Oswegatchie

30 Grassy Pond

Path
2.8 miles round trip, map VIII

The path that leads to Grassy Pond forks left from the Moynehan Road at 0.2 mile. In less than 100 yards it leads to the river, where you may have a slight problem. The metal bridge that formerly spanned the river is now lying unhelpfully across the road. You can cross the river here. The lessee of one of the camps fords it with a four-wheel drive vehicle and will continue to until 1991. If the water is low enough, you can cross on foot without getting too wet.

Across the river, the path circles around and arrives at the north shore of Grassy Pond at 1.4 miles. Grassy Pond is rather shallow; its outlet empties into Sand Lake and is only 2 miles from the boundary of the Five Ponds Wilderness.

West Branch Oswegatchie Trail to Jakes Pond

31 Upper South Pond
Path
2.6 miles round trip, map VIII

Another fork from the Moynehan Road leads to Upper South Pond, one of three remote lakes that are drained by the same creek. All except the lower portion of Upper South Pond were previously in the Forest Preserve, but quite inaccessible to the public until the purchase of Watson's East Triangle. To a degree, it is still inaccessible today.

The trail begins 0.6 mile along the Old Moynehan Road at a point where the logging road goes to the left. At 0.4 mile, along this road, you cross the Middle Branch of the Oswegatchie on a bridge. At a fork at 0.8 mile, turn left. You see Upper South Pond at 1.3 miles. Hemlocks make an impressive sight as they guard the lower portion of the lake. Beaver have flooded the inlet, and the resulting wetland is a typical peat bog.

From Upper South Lake, you can bushwhack to Lower and Middle South Pond in the Five Ponds Wilderness, as remote destinations as you can find in the Forest Preserve.

32 Canoe Routes in Watson's East Triangle
Maps VI, VIII, and XV

The acquisition of Watson's East makes possible several canoe routes, though some of them require long carries before you can start. Included are a few ponds that are close to roads.

1 – West Branch of the Oswegatchie. Put in, with caution, from the Jakes Pond Trail parking lot, section 33, at the shelving area above the waterfall, a carry of about 100 yards. You can canoe for about 1.2 miles of flatwater upstream between the alder-spruce floodplain to the footbridge over the river. Look for azaleas in season.

2 – Middle Branch of the Oswegatchie. This section is known as Alder Bed Flow. The carry or lining down rapids to reach this flow are too difficult for all but a few, but the 14-mile round trip actually does attract a few intrepid paddlers. Access is from the Main Haul Road at a point called High Landing, approximately 9.8 miles from the gate at Bergrens. High Landing is a steep gorge with the river winding below; it formerly was a landing area where logs were put in the river to be floated downriver to a jack-works located near what is now the Alder Bed Flow. You not only have to negotiate the steep, slippery, balsam-covered slope, but you have to carry for nearly 2 miles around rapids to reach the flatwater of the flow, where the river is wide and meandering. Alder Bed Mountain rises above the floodplain. You can enjoy a slow, winding, 8-mile round-trip paddle with only an occasional beaver dam or downed tree.

3 – Moynehan Flow. This artificial flow is the farthest upriver and was made by a dam built at the turn of the century. Put-in is at a spot on the Old Moynehan Road, 1.5 miles from the south gate on the Haul Road. Although the river channel is narrow here, you can paddle for nearly 2 miles above the remnants of the old dam.

33 Jakes Pond
4.1 miles, red trail markers, map VIII

Currently, this is the only marked trail in Watson's East Triangle. It reaches Jakes Pond, which lies cradled between ridges in a formerly isolated, older tract of Forest Preserve. Because of extensive beaver work, you may have to restrict your hike to the first 3.4 miles, after which flooding becomes particularly bothersome.

Access to the trail is a 100-yard spur from the Long Pond-Belfort Road, 0.1 mile short of its terminus at the gate and the beginning of the main haul road.

The first 1.6 miles of this trail is an easement through private land. Follow the red snowmobile markers from the parking lot, crossing the West Branch of the Oswegatchie on a rickety wooden bridge, just at the point where the river funnels into a waterfall and plunges twenty feet over bedrock. There was formerly a dam here which created a flow to aid in floating logs to the mill.

At 1 mile, the trail crosses the West Branch again on a somewhat more substantial wooden bridge. Dead conifers alternate with live spruce and fir here. After a wet crossing of an old beaver flow at 1.1 miles, the trail reaches the fresh markers of the state land survey at 1.6 miles.

The trail crosses ridges of evergreens interspersed with wetlands of marsh grass and balsam fir and tamarack. Sloping outcrops of bedrock are common. At 2 miles there is an intersection: the trail left, the Keck Trail, headed to hunting camps in the vicinity of Buck Pond but it disappears after 0.7 mile in a beaver-flooded morass.

Take the right fork and cross the West Branch again on a wooden bridge at 2.2 miles. Large poplar and aspen—favorite foods of the beaver—occasionally impede travel on the trail.

At 2.5 miles, you cross another old beaver flow—it was a pond as recently as 1986, but has already returned to marsh. Go on to cross a pine-fringed wetland on old corduroy at 2.8 miles. Cotton sedge and tamarack mark the boggy condition of this wetland.

The first serious beaver flooding occurs at 3.2 miles. It may be possible, but it is certainly difficult, to cross on the beaver dam, but you should expect to get wet. If you can cross, or make the long and difficult bushwhack around the flow, the last 0.9-mile walk to Jakes Pond follows the trail along the abandoned road again. This magnificent trail ends at the pond, which is an elongate body of water, encircled by steep, curving ridges that are topped with hemlock and white pine.

34 Middle Branch Oswegatchie Tract
Map VIIIa

A three-cornered acquisition involving the Nature Conservancy, Lassiter Corporation—which recently purchased 96,000 acres from Diamond Inter-

Map VIIIA: Sections 34-35
Based on USGS 7½' Oswegatchie SW and NY
State DOT 7½' Soft Maple Reservoir
Quadrangles.

— — — Trail
— · — · Path
Ⓟ Parking

0.5 mile

national—and the DEC was completed in early 1989. The Middle Branch Oswegatchie Tract, which lies northwest of Watson's East Triangle, is a portion of that acquisition. The tract contains 16,700 acres acquired in fee and approximately 17,000 acres on which the state holds an easement. Existing sporting clubs have a thirty-year period during which they retain exclusive hunting rights, but the public now has all other recreation rights, including fishing.

Access to the tract from the west is described in section 107, the Jadwin State Forest. Access from the south is along a main haul road that forks north from the Belfort-Long Pond Road at a point approximately 0.5 mile from the gate at Bergrens. The road is just before the buildings of the Scout Camp belonging to the Future Farmers of America.

The road, called Bald Mountain Road, crosses Trout Pond Outlet, which is the West Branch of the Oswegatchie River, on a long wooden bridge, then forks left to a gate. The Diamond-Lassiter lands are about 0.5 mile from the bridge. The road continues north through these lands then angles east through a tract for which the state has no easement. Bald Mountain Road is a good gravel road, and it is anticipated that the state will build a road or trail to connect with the Bryant's Bridge Road, which leads to the village of Harrisville. This will permit access from the south to the whole northeastern part of the Middle Branch Tract, with its numerous ponds. Since all of these lands will continue to be logged, be careful near any timber-harvesting operations.

35 Trout and Rock Ponds
Fishing, map VIIIa

A fork just before the gate to the Diamond-Lassiter Oswegatchie Tract leads to two splendid glacial bodies of water—Trout Lake and Rock Pond. Both are encircled by rock cliffs, crowned with towering white pine and hemlock, and are open to the public for fishing only under a cooperative agreement between the DEC and Future Farmers of America. The northern shores of Trout Lake are now part of the Diamond-Lassiter conservation easement.

Aldrich Pond Wild Forest

LIKE THE CRANBERRY Lake area to the east, this region was and to a certain extent remains the domain of the woodsman. But, while the woodsmen associated with Cranberry Lake were primarily the solitary trapper and guide, the Aldrich Pond area is more identified with men wielding crosscut saw and axe.

Aldrich Pond was created by a dam built across the Little River at the turn of the century both to furnish power for a sawmill on the river's bank and to create an artificial lake to hold the logs transported to the mill. At its peak early in the century, the bustling hamlet of Aldrich possessed a school, two churches, and several hundred homes clustered around the mill. As the virgin timber disappeared, the mill was abandoned and the loggers moved on to greener pastures. All that remains today are the foundations of the old mill, the remnants of the breached dam, and the schoolhouse that is now used as a hunting camp.

Also remaining is the bed of the old logging railroad built by the Newton Falls Paper Company to transport logs from the Middle Branch of the Oswegatchie to Aldrich. Today it serves as the route of lengthy snowmobile, horse, and hiking trails described in this chapter.

The pattern of exploitation and subsequent decline of the resource was repeated in the western part of the Aldrich Pond Wild Forest where the Mecca Lumber Company built a sawmill in 1903 and established the hamlet of Kalurah. Kalurah's intriguing name came from the Masonic Lodge in Binghamton. Here too a school and church were built and a logging railroad was extended east to pierce the heart of the uncharted forest. The Mecca Lumber Company left the area for New Hampshire in 1910. All that remains is a cluster of hunting camps and the bed of the railroad that runs from Kalurah to Round Lake.

The nearly abandoned hamlet of Jayville had a somewhat different history. It, too, was the location of an early sawmill; but its zenith occurred when iron mines were opened nearby. Ore extracted from open pit mines was shipped by rail to forges throughout the region. The mine closed abruptly in 1888, partly because of the opening of the more productive

Benson Mines scarcely twenty miles away. During World War II, test borings were made at the site, but the mines were not reopened. A few of the open pits are still present today, mute and hazardous reminders of this bygone era.

In 1920 and 1924, the state began making purchases in this area and the focus of the forest inevitably changed from timbering to conservation and public recreation. As this chapter details, recent additions to the Forest Preserve significantly enhance that recreation.

36 Aldrich to Streeter Lake

Road to drive in summer, cross-country ski or snowmobile trail in winter
4.8 miles one way, maps IX and X

A very pleasant ski excursion uses the road to Streeter Lake, which follows the bed of one of the area's numerous abandoned logging railroads. Skiers will usually find a packed snowmobile base so they can avoid breaking trail. Although the entire route is through Forest Preserve lands, the road is open to vehicular traffic in summer because of a remaining private inholding, the Schuler family mausoleum.

To find the start of the road, turn left at a blinking light on NY 3, 2 miles west of the village of Star Lake in the hamlet of Oswegatchie. Immediately turn left again; you will see Coffin Mills Road on the right. Follow it south for 3.2 miles.

Begin skiing on flat grade, passing the canoe put-in at 0.3 mile on the left. Here, scenic views spread out before you on the left of the Little River flood plain and valley. You pass the trailhead for Round Lake (section 39) and the Wagonbox Trail (section 40) at 1.5 miles. A spruce-fir flat follows, a good place to spot that Adirondack ghost, the snowshoe hare, with its winter mantle of white. Next, a wooden bridge crosses Mud Creek at 1.8 miles, where there is a panoramic vista of the Mud Creek valley and wetland.

Beyond Mud Creek, the grade begins to rise slowly and steadily, passing a steep cliff on the right while a steep narrow ravine drops away to the left. The grade levels off in a marshy vly with an abandoned beaver lodge on the far side. Next, at 4.5 miles, the road turns sharply left where the gate of the Schuler Estate stood. The hardwood cover accounts for the fact you see so few deer here in winter, a contrast with most other ski outings in this guide.

Ski 0.3 mile downslope from the old gate to a metal barrier at the outlet of Streeter Lake. You can explore Streeter Lake (see next section) and return from here, but the truly venturesome may ski on past the barrier for another 6 miles to the Middle Branch Loop (section 37) and return. Alternately, if you have arranged a second vehicle, you have the option of skiing and arriving out on Youngs Road in the village of Star Lake in another 4 miles (section 43).

37 Middle Branch Oswegatchie Loop
Snowmobile and horse trail, canoeing, cross-country skiing, hiking, exploring, discovering the Great Corner
12.3-mile loop, maps IX, X, and XV

A highly scenic, partial loop trail, which provides insight into the early human history of this now quite wild area, begins and ends at Streeter Lake. On the way it explores the remote hinterlands of Herkimer County, several enchanting ponds, a varied galaxy of boreal wetlands, and the secluded Middle Branch of the Oswegatchie River at two widely separated points along its course. The possibilities for further exploration along the way are legion, limited only by the hiker's imagination.

The loop begins at the barred gate by the outlet of Streeter Lake. This is also an ideal place to launch a canoe and explore this attractive lake. There is a lean-to, situated on the eastern shore, which has an idyllic setting. Streeter Mountain hovers above the lake. Take care not to disturb the pair of loons that nest here.

At 0.1 mile, the trail passes through a large field, the site of the former potato fields of the Schuler inholding, which was sold to the state in 1976. The Schuler family fortune was made in potato chips and this remote field was used to raise their experimental seed potatoes far from the ravages of the Colorado potato beetle. The exotic Norway and white spruce planted along much of the perimeter of the field evoke Central Park rather than the Adirondack Park. The fields themselves had their soil structure destroyed by this intensive agriculture and even today, twenty years after they were abandoned, the fields are covered with a thick layer of moss, which inhibits the colonization of the area by grasses and forbs. Grey birch

Map IX: Sections 36-44
Based on USGS 7½' Oswegatchie, and
Oswegatchie SE, Oswegatchie SW and NY
State DOT 7½' Fine Quadrangles.

- - - - Trail
〓〓〓 Bridge
≈≈≈ Canoe Route
-·-·- Path
········ Bushwhack
Π Shelter
Ⓟ Parking

N

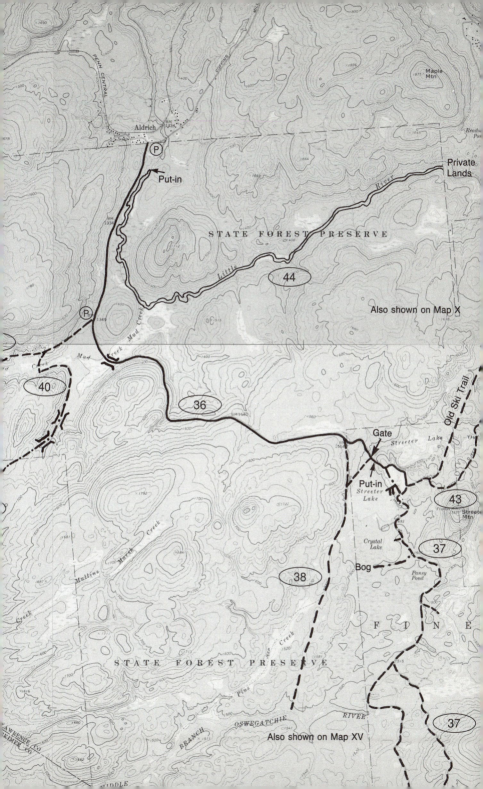

Aldrich

Private
Lands

Put-in

S T A T E   F O R E S T   P R E S E R V E

44

Also shown on Map X

40

Mud Creek

Mud Creek

36

Old Ski Trail

Gate

Streeter Lake

Put-in
Streeter
Lake

43

Streeter
Mtn.

Crystal
Lake

37

Bog

Panny
Pond

38

Mullins Marsh Creek

F I N E

S T A T E   F O R E S T   P R E S E R V E

OSWEGATCHIE   RIVER

37

Also shown on Map XV

and aspen have begun to seed in directly from the adjoining woodlands and this heralds the inevitable return to the forest, which ultimately awaits the field.

Walk across the field, following a path through the moss, or take a longer eastern loop via the old road. The lean-to is off to the right on the lakeshore at about 0.6 mile. Before the state acquired the tract, the main lodge and several outbuildings stood near here. Their foundations lie ahead and to the right of the trail.

An interesting sidelight to life here in the 1940s and 1950s are stories of how the caretaker and his crew, accomplished woodsmen all, captured bobcat kits in the autumn and kept them alive in cages through the winter until spring, when representatives of various circuses and zoos purchased them. You can still find the remains of the cages; but needless to say, this practice is not allowed under the current conservation law.

The trail goes right at a junction at 0.9 mile and shortly beyond goes left at another junction. At 1.1 miles, a short spur to the right leads to Crystal Lake. The Schulers used this lake for swimming and they even created a private beach from sand imported from the Niagara Region. The lake, outlined by a circling ridge, is absolutely clear; its warm, limpid waters are naturally acidified and generally lifeless.

Just beyond the fork to Crystal Lake, a much overgrown logging road goes off to the right. Following it for 0.3 mile will take you to the edge of a large, open peatland, locally known as Streeter Bog. This peatland is an opportunity to spot some of the boreal species of birds: Canada jays, northern three-toed woodpeckers, and ruby crowned kinglets, among others.

At 1.6 miles, the trail passes the outlet of Pansy Pond. The pond itself, reached by a wet bushwhack, is a tiny, peat-lined jewel lying in a kettle hole left in the wake of the receding glacier. The bog mat surrounding it supports a growth of black spruce and tamarack.

Continue on the trail. An old road comes in on the left at 1.8 miles. Going 0.2 mile down it takes you to the banks of Tamarack Creek, just past where it has been joined by the waters of Little Otter Pond Inlet. Due to a quirk of bedrock structure and widening by beaver dams, the creek here in the floodplain is wider than downstream, despite the influx of several more ponds joining along the way.

At 2.3 miles, the trail bears right at a junction; the left fork goes over a shoulder of Francis Hill and rejoins the main trail in 1.7 miles. It is used as a leg of the return loop. At 2.7 miles, you reach the Middle Branch of the Oswegatchie at a point where it makes a wide loop framed in an almost savanna-like setting of balsam fir spires thrust up from grass and sedge openings. It is 1.5 miles from this point downriver to the site of the old Jack-Works, where logs were taken out of the river and transported via the Newton Falls Railroad to the mill at Aldrich. It is also 4 miles upriver from here to the next trail crossing, which this loop eventually reaches. For the next mile, the trail proceeds through a setting of varied conifer woodlands, mostly red spruce and balsam fir, with some hemlock on the glacial knolls. (The latter are an indicator of well-drained swamps, as opposed to peatlands.) It takes you around several beaver ponds, both inactive and active, until you reach a stand of pole-sized hardwoods, just before the trail over Francis Hill rejoins your route at 4.2 miles. You have been following blue horse trail and red snowmobile markers so far; sporadic orange snowmobile markers denote the trail over Francis Hill.

Shortly beyond, at 4.2 miles, the trail crosses Bassett Creek on a wooden bridge. The creek flows into the Middle Branch of the Oswegatchie and downstream its entire length is lined with alder flats and a number of active beaver lodges. At 4.4 miles, there is an old log landing, where logs were skidded and removed by truck to the mill, after the railroads were removed.

From here, follow the blue and red markers straight ahead on a recently marked trail. On the way, cross through heavily cutover hardwoods. At almost 5.5 miles, in a wide open swamp, a very wet stretch of trail is encountered. First there is a stretch of holes and hummocks, ideal for a turned ankle when the grass is high. After this, an improvised walking stick will be a real help in negotiating slippery corduroys and associated pools.

At 5.6 miles the trail comes to a clearing once occupied by Bassout's hunting camp. In addition to the remains of the lodge, with its prominent stone fireplace, there are remnants of other buildings. From the Bassout clearing the trail continues south, now on blue markers only. Just beyond the third marker look for the now collapsed and somewhat camouflaged remains of a hunting camp on the right. This landmark is close to the Great Corner, still out of sight in the forest. This is the northwest corner of the huge colonial Totten and Crossfield Purchses.

From the Great Corner also radiate three of the original Great Lots of the Macomb Pruchase. In 1772, surveyor Archibald Campbell came up from the southeast along a sixty-mile survey line that established the west boundary of Totten and Crossfield. He marked the corner "XLIII AC 1772" (for Township 43). Here he turned east and, for 27 miles, laid out the north line of Totten and Crossfield as far as the shoulder of today's

Coney Mountain; on the way he passed close to Cage Lake, Five Ponds, and High Falls, possibly not realizing that any of these existed.

In 1878, Verplanck Colvin retraced Campbell's west line north from the Beaver River, finding and remarking the Great Corner, as he described in his *3rd-to-7th Report*. He placed a massive and picturesque corner monument at the Great Corner, which today is marked by a blunt-pointed, granite monument placed by the state's careful 1903 resurvey of the entire north line.

From the collapsed camp, pacing off about 500 feet in the forest at 135° (true) by compass will take you to the Great Corner monument with its associated witness trees and an arrow-cut boulder from Colvin's survey in 1878. If you continue following at 90° and 150° along old cut blazes or faded paint blazes, you will be following the Totten and Crossfield north and west boundaries. The Macomb lines at 270° and 300°, however, are easier to follow.

As it passes the collapsed camp, the blue-marked trail is heading due east. About 350 feet from the camp, a grotesque natural marker is found at the right edge of the trail—an uprooted tree stump. The second blue disc from the camp is about 25 feet short of this stump. These details are important, as the Great Corner monument is due south of this disc, in the forest and about 350 not-too-easy feet off the trail.

At 5.7 miles, the trail crosses into Herkimer County and land recently acquired by DEC as part of the Watson's East Triangle purchase. The usual contrast between old Forest Preserve land and most recent acquisitions is not in evidence here as this remote corner was not logged heavily prior to the state acquisition. The trail continues following blue markers until, at almost 6.2 miles, you reach the Middle Branch of the Oswegatchie again at an old ford. Horses have no problem with the ford, but unless you wish to wade chest high at least, further progress is blocked here. Beyond, on the far side of the river, is a labyrinth of interconnecting logging roads penetrating the Watson's East Triangle. These eventually reach the main haul road (sections 28 and 34).

For now, be content with the balsam- and pine-scented breezes from the river. Tarry awhile, enjoy, and reflect. The rather large clearing across the river was the site of one of the lumber camps that once dotted the river; a mile downriver was the site of Maple Hill Flow, one of the impoundments used to flood logs to the mill. Upriver, the Middle Branch is now all in the Forest Preserve to its source at Walker Lake, deep in the Five Ponds Wilderness.

Francis B. Rosevear at the Great Corner

Return via the same route for 2 miles to the junction with the trail going over Francis Hill. That fork is 8.2 miles on your trek. This time continue straight on the trail over Francis Hill, a walk that involves a slow ascent of a shoulder of the hill, followed by an equally slow descent into a large open peatland, which appears just before the two trails rejoin at 10 miles. In late summer, tassels of cotton grass wave above Labrador tea, leatherleaf, and bog laurel. Pitcher plants, scattered in the sphagnum, and tamaracks struggle to gain a foothold on the bog mat.

After the two trails rejoin, follow the blue markers and continue back to the gate, near the outlet of Streeter Lake, for a total loop of 12.3 miles. Long though it is, easy hiking and the boreal scenery make this a pleasant and informative trip.

38   Maple Hill Road

Path along a seasonal road, cross-country skiing, river views
4.4 miles round trip, maps IX and X

Until quite recently, a marked snowmobile trail headed from the gate at Streeter Lake on the continuing bed of the lumber railroad for 3 miles to the spot on the Middle Branch of the Oswegatchie called the Jack-Works. Here logs were taken out of the water after being floated downriver in the spring, to be transported to mills, in this case at Aldrich or beyond. Alas, beaver have inundated the entire latter portion of this trail by building a series of dams along Pins Creek; and now even the remains of the old logging railroad—ties, switches, and so on, which were left after logging ceased in the 1920s—have been underwater for nearly a decade.

However, there is an alternate route to the Middle Branch from the old gate at Streeter Lake, over Maple Hill (local name, not the larger Maple Hill that is beyond the Middle Branch on the county line), to a point on the river approximately 0.5 mile east of the Jack-Works. Maple Hill Road is open to four-wheel-drive vehicles—its rutted depressions attest to that use. Turning right from the gate, the road skirts the shore of Streeter Lake for the first 0.5 mile. You may glimpse the resident loons in summer, but to see the magenta-colored rose pogonia orchid in the open peat mats surrounding Streeter Lake, you should put in a canoe and explore the outlet bay.

There is a spruce-fir and tamarack swamp to the left of the road and beyond this wooded swamp lies one of the larger open peatlands of the park—Streeter's Bog. Canada jays are common here, gliding on silent wings across the open bog.

At 1.2 miles, there is a split in the roadway. Straight ahead leads to the floodwaters of Pins Creek. Going left, the road begins to climb slowly up a ridge crowned with black cherries, many of them lying flattened by windthrow.

The road crests a hill and then makes a rather sharp descent to arrive at the river at 2.2 miles. An overgrown log road winds downstream along the shore of the river to the Jack-Works in about 0.5 mile. This road continues on to reach one of the Diamond-Lassiter tracts recently acquired by the state.

39 Round Lake from Aldrich

Snowmobile trail, cross-country skiing
6.8 miles round trip, map IX

Nestled deep in the Forest Preserve, Round Lake is a large, attractive body of water that can be reached from two different directions by hiking over marked snowmobile trails. The snowmobile trail makes it one continuous route by using the frozen surface of the lake, but unless hikers can walk on water, they should consider the trails as separate. Any connecting bushwhack would be through a miserable wetland around the north shore of the lake. One end of the nearly 10-mile through-trail is on the Aldrich-Streeter Lake Road; the other begins in the abandoned lumbering hamlet of Kalurah.

The Round Lake Trailhead is 1.5 miles south along the approach to Streeter Lake from Aldrich. Park carefully on the right here, where signs indicate. The trail heads through an attractive mixed forest of yellow birch, red maple, red spruce, and hemlock to the junction with the Wagonbox Trail at 0.5 mile. Midway to the junction, in a slight hollow to the left, a magnificent balsam-fir close to one hundred feet tall stands in the midst of other tall conifers. This is close to the maximum size for this species—a unique combination of soil conditions and microclimate probably sends growth here spiraling upward while keeping the tree's diameter quite modest.

After bearing right at the junction, the next 0.8 mile of trail samples some interesting semi-wet areas—crossing over three small wooden bridges that span headwater brooklets of Mud Creek and passing a beaver pond on the left that has started the process of reverting to a wetland. At 1.3 miles, past the last bridge, the trail has been rerouted. It now angles left following yellow discs and begins a slow climb up a rather steep ridge. (The red discs go right through an extensive spruce-fir swamp where perennial flooding has limited the trail's value for hiking, although you may ski on the snowombile-packed base in winter, as it is the preferred route for winter travel. See section 41, Long Lake Loop.)

The ridge has suffered extensive blowdown but still supports many noble specimens of sugar maple and beech, the latter scarred by bear claws. As the trail begins a descent from the ridge, at about 2 miles, several dainty waterfalls brighten the way. Shortly beyond, on a rather small, level mini-clearing, are the crumbling remains of old stone walls and a foundation that may have been either a lumber camp or a camp for tanbarkers who stripped the hemlock bark for use in the tannery at Fine.

The trail now descends to cross Fish Creek at 2.4 miles on a wooden bridge, just at the point where the creek flows out of Long Lake. With the recent Diamond-Lassiter acquisition, the far side of Long Lake is now in the Forest Preserve.

After leaving Long Lake, the trail begins a slow ascent up another long ridge crowned with large hardwoods. An equally gentle descent takes you to the shores of Round Lake at 3.4 miles. A protective cover of hemlock towers over blueberry patches along the shoreline here at an excellent campsite. The lake has brook trout, loons, quiet, and solitude. Directly across the water is the terminus of the Kalurah-Round Lake trail.

40 Wagonbox Trail

Snowmobile trail
1.1 miles, map IX

A short, marked snowmobile trail currently provides the best general access to the Middle Branch Oswegatchie tract, which is one of the newly acquired Diamond-Lassiter tracts. The red-marked route is named after an old logging conveyance used to transport supplies to the area's lumber camps.

Forking from the Round Lake Trail, at 0.5 mile, the Wagonbox Trail crosses Mud Creek Flow on a small wooden bridge and continues along the flow to the former Diamond lands. A fringe of wetland in the form of a spruce-fir swamp is on the left, while a slope with rock ledges protruding rises above the trail on the right.

Beyond the wetland, the trail begins to rise slowly, crossing the creek twice on small wooden bridges. At 0.8 mile, there is a notable specimen of yellow birch, which germinated in moss on top of a large glacial erratic, then extended its roots down to the ground beneath the rock—a growth habit that is typical of the species. At 1.1 miles, toward the top of a long slope, you reach the Diamond Lands.

Interesting here is the sharp contrast between Forest Preserve and managed forests, though most environmentalists believe each has its own particular niche in the Adirondack tapestry, the one complementing the other. The large hardwoods remaining in the clearing have been left standing as seed trees for the emerging hardwoods that now lie under a blanket of berry thickets.

As this is being written, the tract is in the process of being transferred from the Nature Conservancy to the state, so details of public access are not yet clear. The trail goes straight ahead to a fork, then several lefts along logging roads will eventually take you to a junction with the Pins Creek Railroad bed in the vicinity of the old Jack-Works on the Middle Branch. A right goes past Long Lake and eventually reaches Bryant's Bridge, where a town road from the village of Harrisville terminates.

41 Long Lake Loop
Path
7.2-mile loop, map IX

Among the state's Diamond-Lassiter acquisition (see section 34 for details) was the fee purchase of a tract that can be explored from the Round Lake Trail and Wagonbox trails (sections 39 and 40). Walk 0.5 mile on the Round Lake Trail, then veer left on the Wagonbox Trail, and follow it for 1.1 miles to the old boundary line between Forest Preserve and the Long Lake Tract. The boundary marks a vivid, even startling contrast in forests, with the most marked changes being in the understory. Increased sunlight available in the logged forests has left thick blackberry brambles and small saplings—good for deer but not for bushwhacking.

Go straight ahead into the new tract on the private log road for another 1.6 miles to a side road that comes in on the right. On the way you pass two of the hunting camps, which will remain for a period of ten years on what is to be Forest Preserve land. Take the road to the right for another 0.8 mile, curving back north to Long Lake, which is on the left under a bluff covered with hemlock. Another camp that will remain for ten years stands here; both courtesy and the law demand that they be left strictly alone.

Just before you reach the lake, you cross Mink Creek. It and the outlet of Long Lake, Fish Creek, are two of the main drainages in the area. The forest surrounding the lake has not been cut as heavily as other parts of the tract. Walk along the shore of the lake for about 0.7 mile to the bridge over the outlet creek. A ridge with mostly open understory circles the lake and makes for generally easy walking here. At the bridge, turn right on the marked Round Lake snowmobile trail (section 39) and proceed back to its junction with the Wagonbox Trail, where the loop for Long Lake started.

If you make the loop in winter, there is usually a snowmobile base. The old snowmobile trail going through the lowlands may be followed for 2 miles back to the junction of the Wagonbox Trail with the Aldrich-Round Lake Trail of section 39. Total distance of the loop back to the Aldrich-Streeter Lake Road is 7.2 miles; if the trail over the ridge is used, it will be a little (0.3 mile) longer but steep enough to be impractical in winter.

42 Round Lake from Kalurah
Marked snowmobile trail
8 miles round trip, map IX

An old railroad bed, which originates in the abandoned hamlet of Kalurah, provides access to Round Lake from the west. The logging railroad was built by the Mecca Lumber Company, which had a sawmill in this once thriving hamlet, founded in 1903 but quickly abandoned when the lumber company moved on to New Hampshire in 1910.

To reach Kalurah, turn south on Kalurah Road from NY 3 at a point 2 miles west of the village of Harrisville. Proceed about 3.5 miles south to the final crossing of an active railroad (three trains weekly between the paper mill at Newton Falls and Carthage). Immediately beyond, the road splits; the way left dead-ends at state land in the vicinity of the abandoned mining hamlet of Jayville. An old blast furnace lies abandoned nearby. It and some open pit mines are legacies of an era of local mining that came to an end when the mines closed in 1888. Currently, there are no trails through the Forest Preserve to these sites, which are hazardous destinations in any case.

The right fork leads in another 1.5 miles to state land. Past the fork, 0.1 mile, a jeep trail takes off left, providing a legal, mile-long right-of-way to state land where there are several informal campsites. Another mile through the Forest Preserve on a trail continuing from this side road takes you to the banks of Gulf Stream. When you have the leisure time, bushwhack upstream along it to the cliffs, locally known as the Gulf, where forces of running water here have eroded the softer, less resistant rock along the stream and resulted in the steep, canyon-like walls you will see here. This striking geologic formation is repeated nearby along the Middle Branch of the Oswegatchie.

Continuing on the main Kalurah Road, you may have to park just short of 0.6 mile farther at a spot just before the road crosses Gulf Stream on a metal bridge. If the continuing Kalurah Road has not been upgraded, this forces you to start hiking here and adds almost a mile to the one-way distance along the trail.

Otherwise, begin the trail at the start of Forest Preserve land, 0 mile, where a gate currently blocks further vehicle access. A large open wetland bordering Cold Spring Brook follows shortly on the right; it is often patrolled by a red-tailed hawk. At 1 mile, a dead-end snowmobile trail goes right for 0.6 mile to end at a state land boundary. Continue walking south through not too exciting stretches of black cherry and red maple forest that is colonizing these lands logged before their 1920 purchase by the state. At 1.6 miles from the gate, you reach South Creek Lake, which has been stocked by DEC with bass and brown trout; the south half of the lake, however, remains private.

The trail takes a course to the east. After almost 2.9 miles of walking, you reach the Scuttle Hole, a body of water in the slow process of reverting to a long, narrow, marshy vly. You cross it at a narrow isthmus and go for another mile through old beaver flows and wet fields. The trail now begins to rise, crossing a moderate ridge with regal specimens of beech trees crowning its top. After a rather sharp descent, you arrive at Round Lake at just short of 4 miles. Across the water is the terminus of the Round Lake Trail from Aldrich (section 39). In summer, it is best to enjoy the lake and return via the same route to Kalurah.

43 Star Lake–Streeter Lake Loop
Marked horse and snowmobile trail
9.2 miles, maps IX and X

This trail provides a basic loop connecting the hamlet of Star Lake with Streeter Lake, although there are several options for varying the route. The loop follows a network of old snowmobile trails recently revamped as horse trails, as well as a semi-abandoned ski trail that links these routes.

The loop may be started from Youngs Road in Star Lake, at the second trailhead on the right, approximately 1.6 miles south of NY 3. The horse trail starts here—at a parking area approximately 0.1 mile west of the road; a red-marked snowmobile trail that you pass at 1.4 miles along the road may be used as an alternate return route. The marked horse trail passes

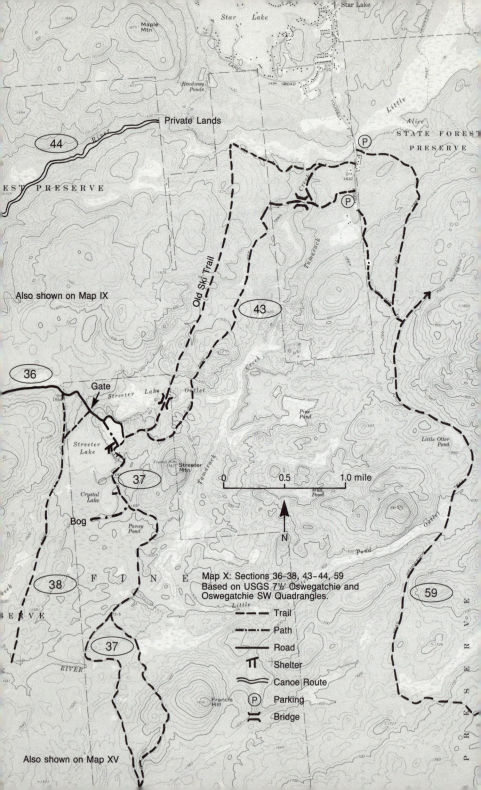

Star Lake

Maple Mtn

Readway Ponds

Private Lands

44

PRESERVE

Also shown on Map IX

Old Ski Trail

43

36

Gate

Streeter Lake Outlet

37

Streeter Lake

Crystal Lake

Bog

Pansy Pond

38

F I N E

37

RIVER

Also shown on Map XV

Little Alice

STATE FOREST

PRESERVE

Tamarack Creek

P

P

Tamarack Creek

Pine Pond

Tamarack

Little Otter Pond

Outlet

Mud Pond

59

0   0.5   1.0 mile

N

Map X: Sections 36–38, 43–44, 59
Based on USGS 7½′ Oswegatchie and
Oswegatchie SW Quadrangles.

Little

– – –	Trail
–·–·–	Path
———	Road
⊓	Shelter
≈≈≈	Canoe Route
Ⓟ	Parking
≈≈	Bridge

Francis Hill

through recently planted conifers to join the snowmobile trail at 0.5 mile. The two trails now combine to cross over Tamarack Creek on a wooden bridge and then begin the start of a slow rise through pioneer balsam fir and an old field of meadowsweet and blueberry until a log road, sporadically marked with red snowmobile markers, comes in on the right, making a sharp intersection with your trail just past the old fields. This trail right is a leg of the return loop. The lands traversed to this point have been recent additions to the Forest Preserve as the old fields and pioneer balsam so tellingly attest.

You pass a rustic hunting camp on a small inholding; and shortly after the trail begins to rise steadily as it veers right at each of two intersections and enters a Scotch pine plantation. The anomaly of this exotic species is explained by the European foresters who influenced American forestry in its formative years, just after the disastrous years of forest fires.

At 1.6 miles, a new wooden bridge crosses an inlet of Tamarack Creek near an old beaver flow. Beyond the flow, the trail begins to get a little muddy, visible evidence that this has been a horse trail since 1987. At 2.7 miles, the trail crosses the outlet of Streeter Lake at a point about 0.5 mile upstream from where it flows into Tamarack Creek and 0.3 mile downstream from where it crosses the Old Ski Trail on the return leg of this loop.

The trail now ascends a shoulder of Streeter Mountain and passes the Old Ski Trail on the right at 3.2 miles. The Schuler potato fields follow at 3.5 miles. Go directly across the opening here to reach the lean-to on the shore of Streeter Lake at 3.7 miles. From it you have a good view of the sharply defined and forested cliffs that line the southern shore.

After a brief rest, return the same way over the potato fields to the yellow-marked ski trail, which heads left at 4.2 miles. Now follow the yellow markers on this old logging road until they turn sharply right into the woods at 4.5 miles. Going straight ahead leads back to the potato fields in another 0.4 mile, passing the bobcat cages and an old gravel pit on the way.

After entering the forest at 4.5 miles, the loop proceeds on a rather narrow ski trail constructed a decade ago by the St. Lawrence County Youth Conservation Corps. A wooden bridge takes the trail over Streeter Lake Outlet in the middle of a spruce-fir swamp at 4.7 miles. The trail weaves through a magnificent hardwood forest with regal specimens of beech and sugar maple highlighting the way. In addition, many glacial erratics of pink granitic gneiss border the trail. The floor under the forest giants is carpeted in early spring with a breathtaking profusion of painted trillium, adders tongue, and spring beauty blossoms.

The trail then heads toward the Little River, which it reaches at 7.3 miles, just at the point where the river is spanned by a long, wooden bridge, quite attractive and quite hazardous! Just before the bridge, a red-marked snowmobile trail goes to the right to reach the snowmobile loop at 8.2 miles, at a point 1 mile from the start of Youngs Road. Turn right, then at 8.7 miles, sharply left to return to your car. Alternately, you can continue on the red snowmobile trail just after you cross Tamarack Creek to arrive back on Youngs Road 0.2 mile north of the horse trail junction with Youngs Road.

The ski trail from the potato patch to the Little River Bridge has been semi-abandoned by DEC, which considers it too difficult for skiing. Trail markers are sporadic, usually about 10 feet high, and the trail is not receiving regular maintenance. The bridge itself had no railings as of 1988, and will be allowed to tumble to oblivion, preventing you from reaching Amos Road in the Village of Star Lake in another 0.8 mile. Still, for the next several years at least, the careful observer can follow the trail making what would be a single route trek through the Aldrich Pond Wild Forest into a more varied loop.

44 Little River
Canoeing
10 miles round trip, maps IX and X

A pleasant canoe trip on the Little River starts from Aldrich and heads upriver. It currently ends in a long set of rapids below a striking waterfall on private, posted property. DEC is presently negotiating for this inholding; and if they are successful, in the future you will be able to continue upriver after approximately a 150-yard carry. After another 2 miles of flatwater, you would arrive at the bridge crossing on Youngs Road in the Village of Star Lake. You will have to surmount a fair amount of downed logs and alder snags in this stretch, particularly after the confluence with Tamarack Creek.

Access to the Little River is 0.3 mile along the Aldrich-Streeter Lake road or ski trail (section 36). There, at a small roadside parking area, a steep 200-foot carry to the left takes you down to the river. The foundation and other remains of the old mill that once sustained the former thriving lumber community of Aldrich are slightly downriver. Put in at one of the two convenient spots close together on the banks and begin paddling upriver.

For the first 2 miles, the river meanders through a wide, marshy wetland with extensive alder swales along its immediate banks. This was formerly Aldrich Pond—a large lake formed by the dam that was erected just below the put-in site. Its sole purpose was to provide water for the lumber industry. With the demise of the virgin forest and the subsequent disintegration of the dam, the river has gradually shrunk back into its original channel, leaving the wetland in place.

Impeded by an occasional beaver dam, especially during the summer, the river resembles the lower Oswegatchie above Inlet in that it shares the same dead-end flows and near oxbows that can temporarily delay the unwary canoeist. Look closely for a running current!

The river was originally named the Little Oswegatchie after its larger, nearby sister into which it flows. The Little River is, today at least, considerably less boreal in its overall aspect than the Oswegatchie. The spruce-fir and giant white pine of the latter are here replaced by alders, marsh grass, and pole-sized hardwoods.

In spring, the mating songs of alder flycatchers, swamp sparrows, and redstarts seem to follow you along the river. Watch for animal footprints on the sandbars—bear, deer, and coyote all visit the river. At just under 2 miles, Mud Creek flows into the river on the right. A mile of paddling and up to a dozen carries upstream on Mud Creek will bring you to the take-out on Mud Creek, on the Aldrich-Streeter Lake Road.

The floodplain ends as Little River narrows just above the confluence with Mud Creek. Upstream, the moderately steep banks flank the river, with occasional intermittent streams draining down through ravines into the river. The current quickens in a few spots. Finally, after about 5 miles, you reach the foot of the rapids and private land. For now, you have to turn about and head back to Aldrich by the same route.

Inlet Road

INLET ROAD HEADS south from NY 3 a mile east of Benson Mines Road. It is a narrow gravel road that winds for 3.2 miles through the Forest Preserve to a secluded point at the DEC parking area that serves as the principal canoe launching site for the Oswegatchie River. For most of its route, the road is the boundary between the Five Ponds Wilderness Area and the Cranberry Lake Wild Forest. In addition to the canoe launch, the road provides access to several relatively little-used trails and paths.

A famous rustic hotel, which catered primarily to sportsmen, once stood on the site of the canoe launch. Called Sternbergs after the first owner, this inholding in the Forest Preserve was acquired by the state in the early 1960s. The hotel was dismantled and nothing remains except a grassy opening in the forest, although there are still a few private camps at the site on both sides of a private footbridge that spans the river.

Scattered Indian artifacts have been discovered at the Inlet Landing, indicating that Native Americans used the landing at least as a temporary camp as they forded the river at this spot. It is presumed that their forays were for moose hunting and beaver trapping, as no evidence has been uncovered of any permanent pre-European settlement.

Inlet Road itself abounds in historical lore. Legend has it that it was the route used by the Tory Sir John Johnson and his followers to flee the Continental Army during the Revolutionary War. This flight began at the loyalists' home in Johnstown, just south of the Adirondacks, and took them to Canada. Later their trail was the route selected for the Albany Road constructed about the time of the War of 1812. It entered the region near the headwaters of the Oswegatchie, crossed the river near the present landing, and terminated at the village of Russell, north of the Adirondack Park. The road proved to be impractical for the transportation of large bodies of troops and it was mainly used by small groups for occasional forays. The road was gradually abandoned so that at the turn of the century it was described as consisting mostly of a stand of sapling yellow birch with the occasional wooden corduroy that had not rotted away. Today even those are gone, but remnants of the road can be discerned.

While Inlet is principally known as the start of the canoe trek into the Five Ponds Wilderness Area (section 62) several trails and paths begin along the road to the landing.

Looking upstream from High Rock on the Oswegatchie

45 Nicks Pond
Path, fishing, camping, maps XI and XIV

A short, 0.1 mile walk over an unmarked path, created by fishermen dragging their canoes, leads you to a thirteen-acre pond. Since most of the Forest Preserve ponds in this region are only accessible by long hikes over marked trails or by relatively difficult bushwhacks over varying, often flooded terrain, this pond is unusual in its accessibility. Large brook trout have been caught here, but if you want to fish, your chances are definitely better if you use a boat or canoe.

To find the beginning of the path, proceed south from NY 3 on Inlet Road for 1.8 miles. There is a pullout for cars on the right and the path is on the left where a small DEC sign points the way. At the end of the short walk, you will see a cliff on the far side of the attractive pond. Hardwood stands around the shores differentiate the pond from those more typical of the region—glacial ponds with conifer-lined shores.

46 Old Wanakena Road
Hiking, cross-country skiing
2.6 miles, maps XI and XIV

A marked snowmobile trail goes through the Cranberry Lake Wild Forest to connect Inlet Road with today's road into Wanakena from NY 3. It has a pleasant, easy grade for summer walking and a rolling terrain that makes for great winter skiing. While you can leave cars at either end to make a one-way trip, it is short enough that you can enjoy the 5.2-mile round-trip from either end. The Inlet Road trailhead is 2.4 miles down Inlet Road from NY 3. The other end is 0.4 mile down Wanakena Road from NY 3.

This old road was the original vehicle road connecting Star Lake with Wanakena, via the Inlet Road. With the building of the modern NY 3 on much of the bed of the Cranberry Lake Railroad, the old route has reverted to a forest trail, though many of the area's older residents can fondly recall driving along this sylvan road in their youth.

The trail is through maturing mixed forest, with patches of beech on some knolls. It passes several overgrown gravel pits that were mined as fill for the road. At 1.7 miles, the marked snowmobile trail has been rerouted for 0.2 mile from the old roadway in order to avoid a stretch often flooded by beaver. At present, the beaver are gone, and you can ignore the detour. This is especially welcome in winter because the climb up the ridge is so steep you will probably have to remove your skis.

At 2.4 miles, the trail joins the Cranberry Lake Railroad bed coming from the Big Fill on the left, and follows it the final 0.3 mile to Wanakena Road, through a Scotch pine plantation.

After the devastating forest fires that occurred in 1908, large areas of this region lay essentially bare of forest cover. Foresters turned to the available Scotch pine to become the miracle tree, which would revegetate the fire-ravaged areas. The presence in this area of the German-born Bernhard Fernow no doubt influenced the choice of this exotic species. Differences in growing conditions and problems with the original seed contrived to prevent the Scotch pine from reaching its full potential as an economic asset in the area.

47 Old Hay Road
Path
6 miles round trip, 3 to 4 hours, relatively level, maps XI and XIV

Approximately 0.2 mile before you get to Inlet Landing, you can spot on the right an unmarked path whose beginning is blocked by boulders. This path penetrates some of the back reaches of the Oswegatchie River and provides an amble along the route of some of the early history of this late settled region. The path is faint in places, but clearly discernible, as it follows a road initially used by early settlers in the Town of Fine to secure wild hay for their livestock in the lush growth carpeting the wetlands along the river and the beaver ponds along the tributary creeks. Later, these haying excursions were lengthened to reach "the Plains," a large treeless area near High Falls. George Sternberg, the original proprietor of the hotel at Inlet Landing, was the last to use the trail as he cut and hauled native wild grasses to feed the few horses and cows that he kept at the landing. The trail was marked as a snowmobile trail by DEC, but is now off limits to vehicles because of its location in a Wilderness Area, thus explaining the boulders at the beginning. The Unit Management Plan for the Five Ponds Wilderness Area calls for resurrecting this route as a marked horse trail, but that has not yet been done.

The path might be called "the way of the beaver," for at many points along its route, members of this rodent family have dammed up small

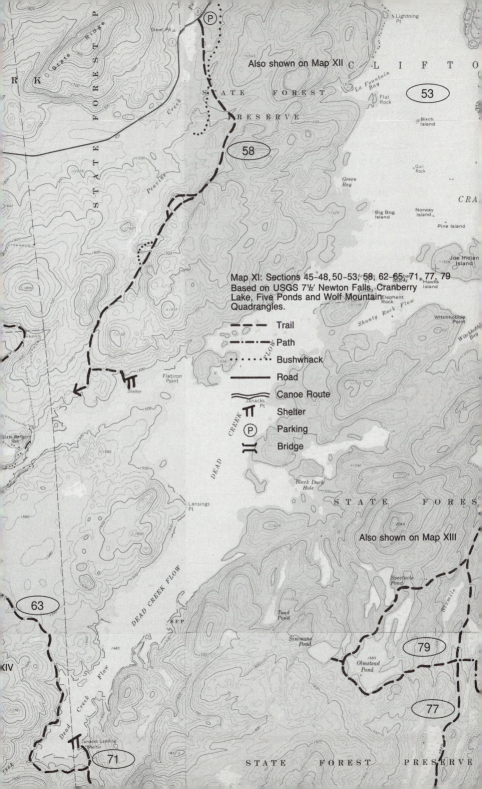

Also shown on Map XII

53

58

Map XI: Sections 45–48, 50–53, 58, 62–65, 71, 77, 79
Based on USGS 7½′ Newton Falls, Cranberry
Lake, Five Ponds and Wolf Mountain
Quadrangles.

- - - - Trail
-·-·- Path
········ Bushwhack
——— Road
〜〜 Canoe Route
ππ Shelter
(P) Parking
)(Bridge

Also shown on Map XIII

63

79

77

71

tributaries of Alice Brook. Their dams are often at the very point where the streams meet the trail, demonstrating the beaver's preference for a slightly elevated and firmly packed base, such as this old roadway, on which to anchor the dams.

The old trail to Alice Brook and Star Lake forks right at 0.3 mile. It is currently flooded by a large beaver pond shortly after it leaves the Old Hay Road path. After 1.6 miles of easy walking, there is another of the ubiquitous Scotch pine plantations. You can bushwhack about 0.3 mile in an easterly direction from the plantation to a parallel series of ridges and ravines that make a pleasing sight as they slope down to the Oswegatchie River.

The path begins a slight descent after leaving the plantation and passes several more small beaver flows on the left. Beaver really seem to prefer the bark of the black cherries, which pioneered the fire-ravaged areas. Notice also how many trees have deformed or broken lower limbs—the consequence of black bears climbing for their fruits.

At 2.4 miles, the path reaches Otter Creek at the site of an old wood and stone bridge, whose remnants are still scattered along the banks here. It was constructed in 1951 to assist in the removal of blowdown timber felled by the hurricane of November 1950. If you could ford the creek here—and generally it is too deep for that—you could, with care, follow the fading path another 1.5 miles as it winds about and finally disappears 0.25 mile from the shores of Otter Pond.

48 Moore Trail

Hiking, river views, fishing, skiing
4 miles, 2 hours round trip, level terrain, maps XI and XIV

This trail is named for Loren Moore, another early proprietor of the sportsmen's retreat that once stood at Inlet Landing. It was used by those early proprietors to reach Wanakena so they could replenish supplies for their out-of-the-way location. It was also used to bring in the sportsmen who arrived by rail at Wanakena. It ambles along the north bank of the Oswegatchie River, providing charming views of the numerous cataracts and rapids that render this scenic section of the river non-navigable.

The trail starts just before Inlet Landing, about 3 miles from NY 3. The beginning is just to the left of the wooden suspension bridge that spans the Oswegatchie, leading to a complex of private camps. The trail crosses a small parcel of private land and winds around wet areas where beaver have dammed streams flowing into the river. Sometimes you have to leave the trail to avoid these small flows, but the inconvenience is compensated by sightings of broods of black ducks and hooded mergansers, who have nested in the flows.

The stand of tall hemlock with occasional red spruce and white pine remains as a concession by the Rich Lumber Company to the early Adirondack guides who worked in the area. The guides wanted large trees left by the river to shade it and keep it cool enough for trout. Arbutus trails along beneath the evergreens and blooms in early spring.

Tumbling rapids alternate with placid pools; sometimes the rushing waters make circular eddies in the resistant rock formations. Early lumberjacks used these pools to wash their clothes; fishermen today use them as points of reference along the river.

At 2 miles, the trail intersects Wanakena Road at a point where it crosses the river on a metal bridge. The Oswegatchie becomes the inlet flow of one of Cranberry Lake's flooded bays shortly after it leaves the hamlet.

49 Otter Pond

Bushwhack, fishing, camping, map XIV

Fifty-acre Otter Pond can be reached by a relatively easy 0.5-mile-long bushwhack along the banks of Otter Creek. Although a logging camp was located close by, the tract containing Otter Pond was essentially left uncut prior to its acquisition by the state in an 1884 tax sale. Consequently, some of the ridges near the pond are clothed with imposing stands of old-growth northern hardwoods. Hoary sugar maples and majestic yellow birches are succumbing with dignity to old age, but enough remain to reward the modest effort required to reach the pond.

The bushwhack begins at a point where the Old Hay Road meets Otter Creek, approximately 2.4 miles from Inlet Road. Hike along the bank of the creek through pole-sized stands of red spruce and balsam fir at first. Then detour around the extensive open marsh that borders the creek. Keeping to high ground as you round the wetland, you notice that the creek is lined with speckled alder and the wetland is filled with blue stem grass, which was the main component of the "poor man's hay" relied on by early settlers as subsistence fodder for their livestock. The few elk present in the Adirondacks also grazed on blue stem grass.

You reach Otter Pond after approximately 1 mile. Just before you see the pond, you cross an inlet creek. If you follow that creek a short distance upstream, you will find a series of three small ponds—the results of glaciers or beavers or both.

The outlet of Otter Pond is dammed by one of the largest beaver dams you may ever encounter. The pond itself is long and narrow—a nice place to camp and enjoy.

For intrepid paddlers, an alternate way of reaching the pond is to canoe up Otter Creek from its junction with the Oswegatchie, which is about 1.5 miles from Inlet Landing. It is about 1.5 miles to Otter Pond outlet, and the reason this is for intrepid paddlers becomes apparent as soon as you leave the Oswegatachie—one expedition encountered twenty-eight small beaver dams to carry over. Exploring Otter Pond by canoe more than compensates for these impediments, however. After exploring the half-mile-long pond, you will find it relatively easy to continue up the surprisingly wide inlet stream for at least another half mile.

New York State Ranger School

A VENERABLE INSTITUTION for three-quarters of a century, known officially as the Forest Technology Campus of State University of New York at Wanakena, the New York State Ranger School has played an important role in the area's history.

The school was originally established to aid the economy of the village of Wanakena after the virgin timber that created the town was all cut. By 1912, the town's founder—the Rich Lumber Company—was moving its mills on to Vermont. The lumber company had purchased 16,000 acres on the southwest side of Cranberry Lake in 1901 and shortly afterwards opened an extension of the Carthage and Adirondack Railroad east from Benson Mines. The line was continued south along the Oswegatchie into what is now the heart of the Five Ponds Wilderness Area and southeast to Dead Creek Flow, an arm of Cranberry Lake. For a brief decade, Wanakena flourished with many lumber camps and settlements nearby, and enough workers to cut all the forests accessible to the railroad in that short time.

The Wanakena campus replaced the first state school of forestry, which was affiliated with Cornell University and was located at Axton, near Tupper Lake. A grant of land from Rich Lumber Company was the beginning and the school has been educating foresters, rangers, and other outdoor technicians since 1915.

The school has created a number of public recreational facilities. Cross-country ski loops use the log roads of the school's forests, though occasionally, when there is active logging, these roads are not available. The unplowed logging roads are open for cross-country skiing in the winter. The trails are marked with various color combinations, but the most useful ski routes are the main haul road system. Marked side trails can also be skied, but they are twisting and narrow in many places. The main routes are the two on either side of NY 3.

50 James F. Dubuar Forest Trail
Nature loop, picnic area
0.5 mile, map XI

Located on the north side of NY 3, approximately 4 miles east of the hamlet of Star Lake, this pleasant picnic grove is maintained by the Ranger School. A short nature trail loops from the picnic area.

The site was a Civilian Conservation Corps Camp from the early 1930s until World War II. Its workers undertook many reforestation projects in the area under the direction of Ranger School personnel. Not only did they create the numerous evergreen plantations, they made many of the area's trails, including the two former truck trails along the railroad beds in the Five Ponds Area. The camp, designated #20 instead of #84, was reopened briefly during World War II, its workers assigned to eradicating gooseberry, the alternate host to the blister rust that was destroying the valuable white pine.

The nature trail is named for a former head of the Forestry School. It heads south from the picnic area and passes ten numbered sites before looping back. Information booklets available at the sign-in booth describe the sites, which highlight various Adirondack trees as well as some introduced conifers and plants of the understory.

51 Ranger School Main Truck Trail Loop
Cross-country ski and snowmobile trail
3.8-mile loop, map XI

This trail begins on the south side of NY 3, 0.7 mile east of its juncture with Wanakena Road, a point that is about 7 miles from the hamlets of Cranberry Lake or Star Lake. You ski the wide log road on a tread that is usually packed by snowmobiles. At 0.2 mile, another log road comes in on the left—it is the return loop.

The trail might be called a forestry practices trail. You ski first past a red pine plantation, which has been thinned recently in a commercial pulpwood operation, then, on your left, past a plantation of Norway and white spruce. Contrast the artificial monoculture exhibited here with the more diverse native red spruce—balsam fir, which is to the right. Especially noticeable in the swamp in winter are the scattered large tamarack festooned with an arboreal lichen—old man's beard, or *usnea*.

You pass an intersection at 0.7 mile, then a narrow side trail, marked with yellow disks, comes in on the left. This short detour returns to the log road trail, but is so narrow it is best done on snowshoes. At 1.2 miles you see a large glacial erratic on the left.

At 1.5 miles, a trail forks left. From the fork you can observe interesting esker formations in the spruce-tamarack swamp. At 2.5 miles, take the log road to the left. (Straight ahead takes you back to NY 3 at a point 0.7 mile from the beginning, for a total trip of 4.2 miles if two vehicles are used. This route is over a natural hardwood slope, followed by extensive pine and spruce plantations.)

The way left begins to descend gradually, with views of the valley to the right opening up. At 2.9 miles, 0.4 along this fork, you can make an interesting side trip to Cathedral Rock. This 0.3-mile spur takes you to an imposing cliff that forms a natural amphitheater with huge angular towers of rock strewn around the bottom of the bowl. For the imaginative, it is definitely a cathedral-like setting; for the porcupines with dens in the rock cliffs, it is home.

Beyond the spur, continue downslope to intersect the road you started on and turn right for 0.2 mile to complete the loop.

52 Crimmins Hill Ski Trail

Cross-country skiing
2.7 miles, map XI

This trail, on the north side of NY 3, begins 0.5 mile west of the picnic area. It ascends the shoulder of Crimmins Hill and at 0.4 mile, a side trail takes off to the left to reach the top of the hill. Well-spaced sugar maple at the top of Crimmins Hill stand in contrast to the red and Scotch pine plantations along the shoulder of the hill. The maples are the school's sugar bush.

The trail goes along a level portion of the hill's shoulder before beginning a fairly steep descent to NY 3 at a point 2.7 miles from the start of the trail, directly across NY 3 from the main truck trail loop. Unless you have a second car at this point, return the way you came.

Cranberry Lake Wild Forest

IN THE LAST century, the name Cranberry Lake conjured the essence of wilderness. It was the most remote and last settled part of the state. The woodsmen who loved its wild haunts—the fabled Adirondack guides and the solitary trappers—left an indelible mark on the area and many remote interior ponds are named in their honor.

The region was the haunt of George Muir, who, with his brother John, hunted for the state bounty the last of the great predators—the panther and the wolf. Muir had a base camp at both Big Deer and Gull ponds. The surveyor Verplanck Colvin met Muir at his "Lost Pond" camp at Big Deer Pond, where Muir gave Colvin directions to Cranberry Lake. Nat Foster, famed trapper from the southern Adirondacks, also hunted in this region.

Prominent naturalists, writers, and artists flocked to the area. The noted naturalist Ernest Thompson Seton stayed with the guide Bert Dobson at High Falls while he pursued the brook trout for which the region was famous. The Canton-born novelist, Irving Bacheller, based his "Silas Strong, Emperor of the Woods" on the prototypical legendary hermit Fide Scott, who also had a hunting camp on Big Deer Pond. The artist Frederic Remington fished and hunted with the local guides and sketched the local scenery, visiting Cranberry Lake every year from 1889 to 1898. Small steamers plied its waters, delivering supplies and mail to rustic hotels and guides' camps.

The region remained relatively inaccessible until this century, when the railroad from Benson Mines reached Inlet. And, it was not until 1913 that the Emporium Forestry Company extended a line, the Grass River Railroad, west from the New York Central near Conifer to the foot of Cranberry Lake. The Emporium Lumber Company owned most of what is now the Cranberry Lake Wild Forest. It sold over 15,000 acres in tracts to the northwest and northeast of the lake to the state in 1933 and 1934, and these tracts comprise two-thirds of the Wild Forest.

Part of the shoreline and a few of the islands remain privately owned, a popular summer colony that began to flourish after 1915. A state campground and a number of campsites line the state-owned shores and a few of these are mentioned in conjunction with the shoreline trailheads that are reached only by boat.

West Flow—Cranberry Lake

53 Cranberry Lake
Canoeing, camping, fishing, maps XI and XII

One of the largest lakes in the Adirondack Park, Cranberry had its surface doubled when its outlet was dammed. The dam, authorized in 1865 and completed in 1867, was built to control flooding and provide a steady source of power to the sawmills and gristmills downstream in the St. Lawrence Valley. The original eighty-foot-long, fifteen-foot-high wood and crib dam was replaced by a higher concrete dam in 1916. That dam has been rebuilt twice since then and continues to provide water for a number of downstream hydro plants.

Before the dam was built, the lake, shaped like an octopus, had its tentacles bordered with peatlands and bogs on which grew the eponymous cranberries. The dam flooded the bogs along the inlet streams and created the long, shallow flows that characterize the modern lake. Last century, fishermen wrote of the desolate shores ringed with dead trees. One bay was named the Hop Yard because its slender tamarack stumps resembled a field of hop poles.

The lake, originally a widening in the Oswegatchie River, had at one time one of the finest brook trout fisheries in the northeastern United States. A combination of factors, including the warming of the water because of the dam and the inadvertent introduction of competing yellow perch, led to a decline in this important fishery. Small mouth bass were later introduced and provided good fishing for a number of years, though lately both bass and perch have declined because of the effects of acid rain. Oddly enough, their decline has led to an improvement in trout fishing, though no one knows if this is more than temporary.

Launch your canoe at the DEC launch site, located on Columbian Road, 0.5 mile south of NY 3. That road is just west of the bridge over the Oswegatchie River. Because the main body of the lake lies open to west winds, it can be dangerous at times for canoes; hence its popularity with motorboaters. Canoes can more safely explore the lake's variety of riches by sticking to the various flows and arms. Many islands dot the lake's surface. The largest, at 91 acres, is Joe Indian Island and it is entirely state owned. The second largest, Buck, is private; but Catamount is also state owned. About three-quarters of the 169-mile shoreline is state owned, providing ample camping opportunities at DEC-designated sites.

While paddling, be on the lookout for some of the abundant wildlife—

the lake has a population of breeding loons that is only exceeded by Stillwater Reservoir and the Bog River Flow. Broods of common mergansers are everywhere in summer. Herring gulls nest on the tiny rock islets where they are safe from predators. Rare for this area are the stands of red pine that grace several headlands. Bear, East, and Indian mountains are the most prominent background features.

A bonus for the canoe camper is access to the vast interconnecting trail network that leads through the Cranberry Lake Wild Forest to the Five Ponds Wilderness that also borders the lake. From the east side of the lake, you can reach Dog Pond Loop and Burntbridge Pond via Brandy Brook Flow, Hedgehog (Clear) Pond via Hedgehog Bay, and Curtis Pond via East Inlet. Trails south of the lake begin from Chair Rock Flow and West Flow, both in South Bay. These trails lead to Darning Needle Pond, Cowhorn Junction, and ultimately to Bog River country. Other trails and loops branch from Dead Creek and Inlet flows.

Brandy Brook Flow sports a colony of houseboats attached to but not touching the shore. Exploring that flow or its elongate tributary, Bear Mountain Flow, is interesting. However, the western flows are more varied. Dead Creek Flow begins just past Joe Indian Island and from the island it is a 6-mile paddle to Janacks Landing at the head of the flow. The large bay 2 miles down the flow was once the favorite haunt of an old-time guide named Rasbeck. Not far away stood Albat's sawmill, named after an early lumber jobber.

On the ridge beyond Black Duck Hole stands a truly wonderful old-growth stand of yellow birch and hemlock, while farther inland in the midst of a stand of white pine is the largest big-tooth aspen to be found in the Adirondack Park.

Janacks Landing has a DEC lean-to and a nice swimming hole nearby. Trails lead from the landing to the top of Cat Mountain and also to High Falls on the Oswegatchie and on to Wanakena. Janack was the first fire observer to man the tower on Cat Mountain and he raised his family at this remote spot.

You can also paddle for a mile or so inside Dead Creek Flow to Inlet Flow. There is another DEC lean-to about a mile up the Oswegatchie on Inlet Flow, at the end of the Peavine Swamp Trail. Monumental white pine tower above the shoreline canopy of this flow, with these old-growth giants ranging up to 150 feet high. The best samples are on the left, just before the head of navigation at the Ranger School about 2 miles up from the lake.

54   Burntbridge Pond Trail

Lean-to, red-marked snowmobile trail
6.7 miles, 3½ hours, relatively level, map XII

The trailhead for Burntbridge Pond and the new Bear Mountain Trail (section 56) begins at the parking area on the south side of NY 3, approximately 2.2 miles east of the hamlet of Cranberry Lake. The trail's route for the first 2 miles or so follows the roadbed of a spur line of the old Grasse River Railroad. Rails were removed from the spur a few years before the state acquired the surrounding tract in 1933.

At 1.4 miles, there is a trail register and the junction with the Bear Mountain Trail. Stay left and shortly beyond, a clearing ablaze in summer with goldenrod marks the site of a lumber camp where twenty-five or so men lived continuously for several years around 1916.

The trail stays along the old roadbed for another mile where it joins an old logging road on the side of a beaver pond. The flooded trees here are a good place to spot tree swallows in summer, while the water below harbors hooded mergansers.

You cross Brandy Brook at 2.9 miles on an attractive wooden bridge at a point near where Barney Burns, one of the old guides, had his camp that catered to brook trout fishermen and nimrods pursuing white-tailed deer. The next grassy clearing you cross on the shores of Brandy Brook Flow is called the Potato Patch—and potatoes were grown here for the region's loggers.

At 3.1 miles, Burntbridge Pond Trail turns sharply left in the clearing—the way straight ahead is the beginning of the Dog Pond Loop. The Burntbridge Trail ascends a long ridge across the head of a ravine, then continues through a hardwood forest with large black cherry and beech trees whose fruits attract bear, deer, raccoons, and grouse in early fall. Sometimes bears cannot wait for the fruit to drop, so their claw marks are clearly visible on the beech bark. The noise made by chipmunks scampering about the dry leaves in October to retrieve the beech nuts would make you think a party of Algonquins had returned to their ancient hunting grounds.

At 5.7 miles, another opening off to the left of the trail marks another abandoned lumber camp, whose foundations are still visible.

At 6.7 miles the trail veers right toward the shores of Burntbridge Pond, where a recently built DEC lean-to occupies a charming lookout under a canopy of red spruce. The site commands a view of the pond with its encircling rim of spruce and tamarack, a place of solitude and quiet well worth the relatively long hike to reach the pond.

The old Lake George Road built in the early 1800s was supposed to have crossed the outlet of the pond on a high bridge, which was burned by Indians in the 1820s. This apocryphal story accounts for the name of the pond, even if it proves to be no more than legend.

55 Bear Mountain from the Campground

6-mile loop, 2½ hours, 675-foot elevation change, red-marked trail, map XII

This 2,160-foot even-topped peak is one of the largest of the area's relatively low mountains. You encounter dense forests as you approach the top, making you wonder if there are any views, but there is a large road outcrop that offers a dramatic view of the woods, waters, and wetlands stretching endlessly to the horizon.

Cranberry Lake itself, with its islands and flows, lies at the foot of the mountain. Among the ring of hills surrounding the lake, the most prominent is Cat to the west with its cliff-like ramparts. To the southwest is the rounded cone of Indian Mountain.

Take Lone Pine Road, just west of Cranberry Lake Village, for 1.3 miles south to the DEC campground. In summer you have to pay an entrance fee. There is a parking area 0.4 mile beyond on the left, where the trail's beginning is marked by a register.

In 0.2 mile, you reach the intersection with the trail from NY 3 (section 56). Turn right into a truly magnificent old-growth forest of yellow birch and hemlock, replaced by equally majestic sugar maples and beech at mid-slope, which shelters the trail. You reach a DEC lean-to on the left of the trail at 0.8 mile. It is surrounded by a stand of white ash. Beyond the lean-to, the trail gets steeper and steeper, with the greatest pitch just before the crest of the mountain at 1.2 miles. Walk the trail along the long ridge until it starts to descend. On the right at 1.4 miles you can see the rock outcrop lookout.

Retrace your steps, or for variety, continue straight ahead to the south, descending steeply to the southeast before curving around the base of the mountain to the west to reach the southern end of the campground at 2.6 miles. Walk north for a mile along the campground roads to your car.

56 Bear Mountain from NY 3

9.6 miles round trip, 5 hours, 660-foot elevation change, red and yellow markers, map XII

A fairly new trail that connects the Burntbridge Pond Trail to the Bear Mountain Campsite Trail now provides access to the top of Bear Mountain without the need to start from the campsite and pay a day-use fee. The trail first crosses the headwater of an extensive wetland on two long boardwalks. Its environs juxtapose old-growth forest with recently acquired land that was logged immediately before its acquisition by the state.

The trail forks 1.4 miles along the Burntbridge Trail near the register. Head right and downslope, on the trail marked with red, and cross a boundary creek on a wooden bridge. Black cherry trees cover the trail, though an occasional large poplar testifies to the age of this pioneering forest.

You cross Bear Mountain Creek at 2.4 miles. Wooden planking takes you over it and its adjoining wetlands. These are typical Adirondack wetlands with open sedges flanked by a spruce-fir forest, occasional tamarack, and even white cedar. The trail crosses a fringe of the upland spruce-fir forest and then reenters the wetland via more boardwalk. This area was known a century ago as Bear Mountain Lake for it was at one time flooded.

At 2.9 miles, the trail turns sharply left and then makes a sharp right turn to go into a more mature forest. It skirts a spruce swamp to the left and passes below a steep cliff on the right to arrive at a connection with the Bear Mountain Campsite Trail at 3.6 miles, 0.2 mile from the beginning of that trail. Turn left on the red-marked trail and follow it for the mile to the summit and on to the overlook (section 55), for a total trip of 4.8 miles.

57 Dog Pond Loop

Combination of new and existing trails
22.5 miles, relatively level, red and blue markers, map XII

DEC has built a wonderful loop trail through the Cranberry Lake Wild Forest, completing the last portion of that trail in 1989. The new blue-marked hiking trail section north from Dog Pond to the Burntbridge Pond

Trail was marked and cut out during the late summer of 1989. The last portion of the loop is along the 6.7-mile red-marked snowmobile trail to Burntbridge Pond.

The loop offers hikers much variety, including several formerly land-locked glacial ponds, a glimpse of a magnificent old-growth hardwood forest, a taste of the formerly trailless shores of Brandy Brook Flow, and even a cavern or two!

The first 3.1 miles of the loop is along the Burntbridge Pond Trail as far as the Potato Patch on Brandy Brook Flow. Here the orange snowmobile disks disappear and you follow blue markers as you continue straight ahead and then swing right. (Burntbridge Pond Trail, the route of the return loop, heads left with red markers. See section 54.)

The trail follows the shores of Brandy Brook Flow for the next 1.4 miles, passing four short, marked spur trails to designated campsites on the flow to the right. At 4.2 miles, you reach the last designated campsite on the flow. A huge stone chimney stands here—a mute and incongruous re-minder of the Indian Mountain Club, an exclusive club for wealthy sportsmen at the turn of the century. Bear Mountain is visible across the flow here, while a large island is prominent at the mouth of Bear Mountain Flow, marking the point where that flow joins the main Brandy Brook Flow.

Four Cranberry Lake houseboats intrude on this almost pristine setting. These houseboats moored to the shores of Brandy Brook Flow have an interesting history. They were built early in the century and are considered legal if they remain over the waters of the lake or the flows but do not at any point touch the adjacent banks, which are part of the Forest Preserve.

At 4.5 miles, the trail turns away from the flow and begins a gradual ascent into stands of dying beech. Large sugar maples also begin to appear as the trail proceeds on the sides of a slope, crossing two ravines on the way to an intersection with the yellow-marked Clear Pond Trail at 5.3 miles. The way right leads in 0.3 mile to the shore of Cranberry Lake. The way left leads in 0.2 mile to the banks of Clear Pond, which is circular and has the imposing bulk of East Mountain rising over it. Glacial erratics, capped with rock polypody ferns, ring the shore.

Clear Pond is called Hedgehog on the USGS, though Clear is the more accepted name. Those boating on Cranberry Lake can intersect the loop trail at this point via a 0.3-mile connector from Hedgehog Bay.

Continuing straight on the loop from the intersection takes you to the north shore of Cranberry Lake's East Inlet at nearly 6 miles. Here a spur trail leads to a designated campsite on the northeast shore of East Inlet.

Map XII: Sections 53–57
Based on USGS 7½' Cranberry Lake and NY
State DOT 7½' Long Tom Mountain
Quadrangles.

- - - - Trail
- · - · Path
⌂ Shelter
≍ Bridge
P Parking

54

56

Silver Lake

Cranberry Lake

Boat Ramp

Chipmunk Bay

Lost Pond

Matilda Bay

Matilda Island

Marina

Green Pt

Dog Island

Thompson Bay

Bear Mountain Swamp

Bear Mtn Flow

ADIRONDACK   STATE   PA

Lightning Pt

Res

Shelter

Cranberry Lake Campground

Bear Mountain

55

C L I F T O N

La Fountain Bay

Flat Rock

53

Union Pt

Burnt Rock

Brandy Brook Flow

Birch Island

Eagle Island

Hedgehog Pond

Spring

Green Bay

Gull Rock

Hedgehog Bay

CRANBERRY   LAKE

Big Bog Island

Norway Island

Pine Island

Sears Islands

Catamount Island

East   Inlet

0   0.5   1.0 mile

Joes Pt

Joe Indian Island

Arnolds Pt

Kimball Island

Hawks Island

Long Pt

Elephant Rock

Shanty Rock Flow

Witchhobble Point

Witchhobble Bay

Deremo Pt

Buck Island

Coles Pt

Barber Island

Barber Point

Cranberry Lake Biological Station

N

Sucker

Boaters can pick up the loop at this point, though for them, a more logical beginning is on the southeast corner of the inlet where a 0.9-mile, red-marked trail leads directly to Curtis Pond.

The loop trail next crosses East Creek and begins to rise. Just before the crest of a sugar maple ridge, you can spot a sign pointing to a spring. The gradual ascent continues with majestic beech trees now joining the sugar maples. At 7.2 miles, you pass a natural amphitheater on the right, a complex of boulders that furnishes dens for bobcats and fishers.

Climb some more, reaching the 1900-foot level. When the leaves are off the trees, you can see Cranberry Lake downslope to the right. Follow the trail through this impressive forest until it meets the red-marked Curtis Pond Trail at 7.5 miles.

You now go left and follow both red and blue markers to arrive at Curtis Pond at 7.8 miles. (Lanson "Lant" Curtis was a trapper who had a camp on East Inlet.) Just before the trail reaches the shore of the pond, the red trail turns right to a natural cave-type shelter that is famous in local lore. The cave, actually two slabs of rock tumbled one over another, reputedly furnished haven to the trapper Nat Foster as he was being pursued by an Algonquin hunting party.

A DEC lean-to is sited across the lake. Relax and enjoy the spruce-crested ridge above the lake, the inevitable beaver dam across its outlet, and the sight of brook trout rippling the placid surface of the water at dusk.

The trail circles the lake, passing a pleasant natural campsite on a white-pine knoll on the far side of the lake. At 8.1 miles you see a steep cliff to the right. The huge talus blocks piled beneath it are an outgrowth of the erosion and weathering that has gone on ever since the last glacier began its retreat.

At 8.8 miles, the trail reaches Willys Pond, which has a fringe of dead timber around its shore. Until construction of this new trail, Willys Pond could only be reached by a bushwhack from Curtis Pond. Looping south along Willys Pond, then east, the trail reaches another pond at 9.4 miles. Irish Pond, named for Jesse Irish, the first permanent settler in the Cranberry Lake Region, was also formerly accessible only by bushwhacking. It is deeper than Willys; a stand of large hemlock overlooks its outlet ravine, and an island graces the middle of the pond.

From Irish Pond, the loop leads east to reach Dog Pond at 10.3 miles. According to local legend, Jesse Irish killed an animal that seemed to be a cross between a dog and a wolf at this pond, so the name of the pond was changed to Dog from Ami. The original name came from Ami Brumley, a noted wolf hunter.

Here, the present end of the trail, the loop will eventually continue north approximately another 4.2 miles to Burntbridge Pond for a total distance of 14.4 miles. Another 6.7 miles on the Burntbridge Pond trail completes the loop.

From Dog Pond, the new blue-marked portion of the loop heads through the draw north of Dog Pond and continues heading slightly east of north, generally paralleling the state land boundary for 4.5 miles of gentle ups and downs. It is a beautiful trail through varied forest types.

The trail intersects the Burntbridge Pond Trail at a point 1 mile west of Burntbridge Pond. Turn east to reach the pond, or turn west to complete the loop. Mileage for the total loop asumes a visit to the pond as part of the loop.

58 Peavine Swamp Trail

Ski trail, old-growth forest, camping
8.4 miles round trip, 4 hours, relatively level, map XI

This trail was constructed recently to serve primarily as a cross-country ski trail. It provides access to a secluded DEC lean-to that lies nestled on the shores of the Inlet or Main Flow of Cranberry Lake. The trail starts on the south side of NY 3, about 100 yards west of the DOT parking lot, which is on the north side of the highway. This point is 1.9 miles west of the bridge over the Oswegatchie in the hamlet of Cranberry Lake. A small DEC sign points the way.

The route of the trail for the first mile has an interesting history. It follows the path of an old "blowdown" road constructed solely to salvage downed timber in the aftermath of the November 1950 hurricane. For several years after the hurricane, the woods were closed to recreationists. The timber harvest, a controversial move, was sanctioned by the State Attorney General's opinion on the grounds that it would reduce the fire hazard of the blowdown.

The trail goes through a spruce-fir flat with occasional knolls and several small wooden bridges spanning creeks that drain west into Peavine Swamp, which the trail skirts, but does not enter. The swamp, actually mostly a bog forest of spruce-fir and tamarack drained by Peavine Creek, is an extensive deer yard in winter. Look for bobcat tracks in winter—they are attracted by the deer and snowshoe hares. Peavine Swamp looms large in local legend as a place to get lost easily or "turned around." In addition to the unvarying flatness and the denseness of the boreal conifers, there are recurring tales of hunters whose compasses failed to function in the swamp, perhaps due to the presence of magnetic iron ore in the underlying bedrock.

After going up and down a few slopes, the trail proceeds through a hardwood forest, distinguished by noble specimens of mature black cherry. At 1.8 miles, a steep cliff to the left is especially noticeable when the leaves are off the trees. Glacial erratics of pink granitic gneiss are common here. The crushed remains of some of them that have been dynamited to push the trail from the end of the old blowdown road occasionally make walking difficult—it is, after all, primarily a ski trail.

At 2.2 miles you climb the crest of a hill with several magnificent hemlock trees, which have recently been measured by local DEC foresters. Specimens exceed 42 inches diameter at breast height, splendid dimensions for a hemlock. Nearby are several imposing specimens of old-growth red spruce, nearly as tall as the hemlock, but in sharp contrast to them because their diameter is barely half that of the hemlock.

The trail now descends through a draw to reach an old tote road at 3 miles. Follow the yellow marker here until at 3.7 miles, you turn sharply left—a sign points the way. The trail ahead goes to the Ranger School in 1 mile. The way left leads in another 0.5 mile through a forest of huge yellow birch and hemlock to a DEC lean-to. The total ski trek is 4.1 miles to this point. The lean-to is tucked under a protective canopy of white pine, just back from the shores of Inlet Flow, about 1 mile from its confluence with Dead Creek Flow. The flow is about 150 yards wide here, a lovely spot to linger before you retrace your steps.

Five Ponds Wilderness Area

SOUTH OF CRANBERRY Lake lies one of the wildest Forest Preserve parcels in the state, the 95,525-acre Five Ponds Wilderness Area. It is an area of topographic transition; the land steadily descends from the prominent mountains on its eastern edge to the lesser hills and glacial outwash basin to the west. Dozens of small lakes and ponds rest between the hills, most of which form the headwaters of the East Branch of the Oswegatchie River. So gentle are the contours that extensive wetlands have formed along many of the waterways, providing important habitat in which many mammals and birds feed, breed, and seek cover. Dense stands of alder, tamarack, and black and white spruce can be found in these slack waters. Everywhere you can see the results of the last glaciation in the eskers that course through the region. These sinuous ridges of sand were deposited by channels of meltwaters of the receding glaciers and are frequently topped by sand-loving white pines.

Much of the northern portion was heavily cutover after the turn of the century and it is dominated by maturing stands of beech, yellow birch, black cherry, red maple, and hemlock. However, the lands to the south, which were incorporated into the Forest Preserve before 1904, were not harvested and a beautiful old growth forest of beech, maple, white pine, white and red spruce, yellow birch, and cedar exists. This area is recognized as the most significant remaining stand of old growth timber in the northeastern United States.

The patterns of trail development, and therefore public use, basically coincide with this condition of the forest. The Red Horse Trail, described in the Stillwater Reservoir chapter, is the only formal trail maintained in the southern section. The situation is quite different in the northern section, where several trails and lean-tos are located. These trails were laid out along traditional hunters' paths and the beds of the Rich Lumber Company's railroads; they reach out in all directions. Access points are concentrated between Star Lake and Wanakena, with additional canoe access from the southern edge of Cranberry Lake and the western end of Lows Lake.

The majority of trails, however, follow in part the routes of logging roads dating to the early part of the twentieth century. When Robert Marshall was a student at the Syracuse School of Forestry, he spent the summer term of 1922 at Summer Camp on Cranberry Lake. Every weekend he walked the roads or bushwhacked between ponds and the small mountains. He chronicled the routes and the horrible mess of slash and burned forests left after the logging. His diary for that summer also includes the etymology of many geographical features, notes which have been used extensively in this chapter.

In recent years, the trail system has undergone significant changes and many trails have been abandoned or rerouted due to the difficulty of maintaining flooded sections. New trails, camping sites, and lean-tos are proposed. The Unit Management Plan calls for abandonment of some trails and removal of some lean-tos to bring the area under wilderness guidelines. Most of the major ponds have been stocked with brook trout, but several of the smaller ponds have a low potential for fish vigor due to high levels of acidification.

59   Boundary Trail and Buck Pond Primitive Corridor

Trail, hiking, cross-country skiing
7 miles, 3½ hours, minimal elevation changes, maps X and XV

With the abandonment of the direct trail to Cage Lake due to flooding, and the washout of the bridge over the Oswegatchie River along that trail, this route from Star Lake to Buck Pond is now the shortest route connecting with trails to Cage Lake (section 60) and the heart of the Five Ponds Wilderness. The trail traverses what is called a Primitive Corridor because it leads to the private inholding at Buck Pond.

To reach the trailhead for the new Boundary Trail, take Youngs Road south from its intersection with NY 3 for approximately 2 miles until you see the boundary of Forest Preserve land on your left, just short of the end of the road. A new trail was constructed here by the St. Lawrence Youth Conservation Corps in 1989. It begins at an unimproved parking area just off the road. The old trail to Buck Pond and Cage Lake began approximately 0.5 mile farther north, diagonally opposite one of the trail beginnings to Streeter Lake. The new trail was constructed because the first part of the old route became impossible to hike as a result of damage by ATVs that were used to reach the private inholding at Buck Pond.

The new trail from the end of the road begins by rising slightly as it crosses a knoll under a mature canopy of handsome hemlock and yellow birch with occasional red spruce. The contrast between this almost old-growth forest and the recently logged private land just over the boundary is quite dramatic. As this land is also being added to the Forest Preserve, that contrast will gradually fade. You encounter some large beech just before the trail meets an old log road at 0.6 mile.

The trail turns left here and begins to ascend again with rutted portions present at dips—still the result of vehicles going to the private inholding. At 1.1 miles, the fork left is the old route out to Youngs Road. That route is 2 miles long, making the trip to Cage Lake via the new trail 0.9 mile shorter.

At 1.3 miles, an old logging railroad bed called the Post-Henderson Road comes in rather sharply on the left. The trail now follows the firm base of the railroad bed south for approximately the next 6 miles, reducing somewhat the ruts encountered on the first portion of the trail.

(You can still make a loop along the railroad bed to the left, veering left at Alice Brook to take a more distinct unmarked trail back to a junction with an old road where another left returns you to the road you have been traveling on. The first 2 miles of this 6-mile loop along the railroad bed is quite overgrown and flooded by beaver, but with care you can still follow it.)

The trail is now marked with both yellow discs and red snowmobile discs as it traverses a mid-successional forest of red maple and white ash. Occasional large brooding specimens of big-tooth aspen or poplar remain from the turn-of-century fires. Apparently these fires were limited to the disturbed lands and were suppressed before they reached the mature forests at the beginning of the trail.

At 2.5 miles you reach thirteen-acre Little Otter Pond, which is surrounded on all sides by emerging hardwoods, with a few large white pines. The pines not only provide a little variety in the forest mosaic, they are a haven for porcupines in winter. Check the ponds for broods of hooded mergansers in summer. The trail continues along the east shore of the pond, and begins to encounter wetlands. It crosses the outlet of Little Otter Pond at 3.3 miles and several tributary streams in a large open sedge marsh fringed with conifers.

Beaver activity for the next 2 miles occasionally floods the trail. The forest now begins to mature somewhat. At 5.1 miles, the old railroad bed you have been traveling forks right and ends in a few hundred yards. The

Map XIII: Sections 12–14, 62–63, 65, 69–84
Based on USGS 7½' Cranberry Lake, Newton
Falls, Wolf Mountain and Five Ponds
Quadrangles.

Trail
Path
Bushwhack
Canoe Route
π   Shelter
⇇   Scenic View
Ⓟ   Parking

Also shown on Map III

trail forks left around a gate barring further unauthorized motor vehicle traffic. You begin to climb again over one of the region's many equal-sized hills, this one covered with impressive hemlock and sugar maples. The slow descent from this hill leads to the shores of Buck Pond, short of 7 miles.

The private camp buildings are at the head of the lake. The forest surrounding the lake is more mature than that at Little Otter Pond. Whorls in the placid surface mark the place brook trout rise to devour floating insects.

Just before you reach the pond, another trail forks right. It leads along the shores of Buck Pond before it zigzags southwest to continue on to Cage Lake, described in the next section.

60 Cage Lake

Trail, hiking, lean-to, swimming, fishing
1.2 miles, 45 minutes (from Buck Pond), easy to moderate grades, map XV

Cage Lake was named for Cage Ackerman, one of the many hunters whose names were given to the region's lakes and ponds. The yellow-marked trail to Cage Lake turns right off the Buck Pond Primitive Corridor at Buck Pond. Leaving private land, you come to a junction at 0.3 mile where the old trail from Cage Lake Springhole on the Oswegatchie River enters on the left. Because of problem flooding on both sides of the river, this 2.4-mile trail was quickly abandoned when the bridge it crossed washed out. The trail is virtually nonexistent now along the 0.6-mile segment in the Oswegatchie floodplain and the Cage Lake Springhole Lean-to on the west bank has become a facility best suited for the canoeing public. The experienced wilderness navigator can still follow the trail's faint tread through a handsome old-growth hardwood forest along the shoulder of a hill north of Buck Brook. A few yellow markers remain, but they are rapidly disappearing. You may wish to walk the first 0.1 mile to see the wetland where the outlets of Buck Pond and Cage Lake combine.

The trail to Cage Lake swings right from the junction and after fifteen minutes you descend to cross Hammer Creek. The terrain is very swampy and the trail has been rerouted in numerous spots. You encounter modest

Cage Lake near the lean-to

ups and downs for the next twenty minutes as you continue on through a mixed woods. A gradual descent takes you to a wetland where the trail has been especially difficult to maintain. A flagged route to the right offers drier walking, but both routes become confusing. You should cross to the other side of the wetland and pick up the trail as it heads southwest. Another five minutes should take you to the outlet where you can find rocks to hop across. The trail then rises up a pitch on the opposite side to the Cage Lake Lean-to, which is in good shape. A path to the left goes to the privy, which is nothing more than a metal seat on a wooden frame. A path to the right leads 75 feet to rocks at the lake's edge where you can swim or fish. The view up the lake is quite attractive. The lake is one of the larger bodies of water in the Five Ponds Wilderness and is bordered on the northwest by steep slopes. Blowdown has broken the maturing red spruce that crown the slopes. In spring, black bears weave paths through the blowdown.

Maintenance of this trail and its continuation to Wolf Pond (section 61) has been poor in recent years and blowdown and undergrowth, combined with the flooding problems, have made travel over the route very discouraging. Fortunately, major trail and facility improvement was started in the area in the spring of 1989 and work in this section should be completed in 1990.

61 Wolf Pond

Trail, hiking, lean-to, camping, fishing
2.8 miles, 1½ hours (from Cage Lake), moderate grades, map
XV

By anyone's definition, this is a wilderness trail! The mixed woods are tall and dense and since you have already hiked almost 10 miles to get here, the grades seem more tiring and the solitude more intense. Blowdown, undergrowth, and wet spots have long been aggravating problems along the way, but as mentioned previously, the scheduled 1989 maintenance should greatly improve the journey.

An old sign on a tree to the right of the lean-to at Cage Lake marks the beginning of the trail to Wolf Pond. Plunging into the trees, you soon begin a steady climb that takes you into a tall hardwood forest on the shoulder of a hill. After one half hour, a gradual descent leads to the outlet of Deer Marsh, which you can easily cross on rocks. Swinging southwest, you follow rolling contours as the trail avoids wet lowlands to the east. After a steady descent, you arrive at the outlet of Muir Pond, which flows through a deep gully. Crossing is not easy and you must use the muddy remains of beaver dams or fallen trees. The trail can be hard to find on the opposite side; look for it off to your right. Muir Pond is named after George and John Muir, two turn-of-the-century woodsmen who hunted wolves and panthers relentlessly in a time when the significance of these majestic predators was not understood. In later years, George, the more efficient hunter of the two, became a caretaker of the Gull Lake Camp at the Webb Estate to the east. One spring he trudged off from Wanakena to make the 12-mile hike through the snow to Gull Lake. He never made it; his body was found in the wilderness south of High Falls. He was eighty years old.

You pass the pond, whose name is a desolate reminder of times past, after hiking for an hour. For the next fifteen minutes, the trail is relatively level, then it drops to the edge of an expansive wetland, through which the Wolf Pond outlet flows. Crossing the outlet has traditionally been over an old 200-foot-long beaver dam. It is a precarious crossing at best and you are more than likely to get wet feet in the process. The scenery is, however, beautiful. Once across, the trail bears left and climbs steadily up a knoll, reaching the lean-to in ten minutes. It has a dirt floor and is in fairly good condition. Wolf Pond is visible down through the trees and a rough path in front of the lean-to drops down to its brushy edge.

The trail continues past the lean-to, passing a campsite on the left and an outhouse on the right. Two more small clearings border the trail before it pitches up to the junction with the Five Ponds Trail, ten minutes from the lean-to.

62 Oswegatchie River and High Falls
Canoe trip, maps IV, XI, XIII, XIV, and XV

The Oswegatchie River, navigable for twenty miles above Inlet Landing, winds a snakelike course into the heart of the Five Ponds Wilderness. Use it to reach interior trails or simply enjoy this wilderness trip highlighted by the sight of two waterfalls. Before you start, read about the loggers' and guides' camps along the river's course as described by Herbert F. Keith in his *Man of the Woods*. Paul Jamieson's *Canoe Waters—North Flow* gives additional details.

Wildlife sightings are frequent as the river meanders through sprawling wetlands. You may spot otter at dusk, you may see beaver swimming silently, and you may even be fortunate enough to see a cow moose and her newborn calf swimming the river. One such sighting was reported three years ago, the first encounter with a native moose in over a century. Osprey frequently soar overhead or dive for the numerous small brook trout. There is an active nest on the upper reaches of the river.

Put in at Inlet, see page 107, where a suspension bridge crosses the river and leads to private lands. A sandy landing on the upstream side of the bank is the put-in. The river has a few riffles, shallows, shoals, and Class 1 rapids, but these are minor inconveniences between long stretches of flat, easy water. What may prove to be greater impediments are the numerous channels and pseudo channels that entwine the main course, confusing your choice of route upstream. In low water, even trying to follow the strongest flow of water may prove difficult. In high water, you do have to contend with a good current.

Because of the river's winding course, mileages are approximate. If you allow a day to paddle to High Falls, at least one day to explore above the falls, and a day to return, you will have a good sample of the river, but you could easily spend a week hiking from interior trailheads and paddling above the falls. The carry, marked by the DEC in 1987, connects the Oswegatchie with the headwaters of the Bog River. This headwaters canoe carry (sections 14 and 83) opens up what is surely the ultimate in wilderness canoe trekking in the entire northeast.

The virgin, or more properly, old-growth, forests for which the region is noted can be easily explored from two spots along the river. In the vicinity of Griffin Rapids and Cage Lake Springhole Lean-to, you can find old-growth hardwoods. Virgin white pine cover Pine Ridge, which is about 2 miles above High Falls. Although the stand is not as majestic as it was before the hurricane of 1950 devastated the region, it is still impressive.

From Inlet, you paddle 4 winding miles upstream to High Rock, where you ought to pause and look out over the Oswegatchie's vast floodplain. There are lean-tos at Griffin Rapids, over 2 more miles upstream, and at Cage Lake Springhole, another 1.5 miles or so farther upstream, where Buck Brook flows into the river. At almost 11 miles you pass Wolf Pond Outlet; the new hiker's bridge and the Five Ponds Trail (section 66) are just beyond. In the next stretch, the river narrows considerably as it winds through swamps sometimes close to the High Falls Trail (section 63). It passes Carters Landing with views north across The Plains.

High Falls, one of the river's two imposing waterfalls, is 13.2 miles above Inlet Landing. The water drops no more than fifteen feet here, but on the

High Falls on the Oswegatchie

sluggish Oswegatchie, that makes it quite high. After a carry of 0.25 mile around the falls, you can canoe as far upstream as the point where the Robinson River comes in on the right. A bushwhack of 5 miles along the bank of the Robinson takes you to the second waterfall, Sliding Falls, which is not as wide as High Falls, but still an imposing sight. Even more rewarding than the view of the falls is the knowledge that this is one of the most remote places in the whole state.

A paddle of about 2 more miles upstream on the Oswegatchie from the confluence with the Robinson takes you to a place called Beaverdam by the old Adirondack guides. Here is the end of the carry from Lows Lake and Big Deer Pond.

If you are camped near High Falls, you can visit some historic wilderness territory south of the river. (The bridge is removed, so canoe access is important.) The St. Lawrence/Herkimer county line, about a half mile south of High Falls, is the north line of the vast and ancient Totten and Crossfield Purchase, a line orginally surveyed by Archibald Campbell. A path along the ridge back of the south-side lean-to and outhouse heads west, then southwest, and finally south. The terrain is flat at first and often soggy. Well-defined stretches are frequently interrupted by blowdowns, and sometimes a little floundering and help from the compass are required before the next stretch of obvious path is picked up. Occasional old axe blazes or faded yellow paint blazes are also helpful. The route is not for casual hikers.

A few rusted trail discs will be seen as the county line is approached; these are from the early-twenties "old ADK yellow trail," of which today's Red Horse Trail (section 20) is a remnant. If you are sharp-eyed and lucky, you can locate the county line by spotting an orange-painted line monument from the 1903 county line resurvey. It is a steel I-beam about 50 feet east of the trail and extending about two feet above ground; it may be partly hidden by undergrowth. Faint yellow paint blazes east and west of the path may be helpful in locating the line. If you come to bright orange blazes, or cross a little north-flowing stream, you have passed the county line.

At one time the Albany Trail from the southeast (sometimes called the "Old Military Road") and the Red Horse Trail from the southwest intersected just south of the county line. The 1903 surveyors placed the I-beam about 75 feet west of the Old Military Road; hence the present path is about 125 feet west of the original trail. Judging by the presence of the rusty discs, the relocation was done during or before the routing of the ADK trail.

West of the path the going along the county line is not difficult. (To the east, swampy ground, heavy growth, and blowdowns are typical.) Westward, the yellow blazes can be followed about 800 feet to the next I-beam at the tip of "The Dagger," the controversial survey gore that extends ten miles to the east. The easier going suggests a possible 1½-mile bushwhack "shortcut" west to the Five Ponds Trail, guiding on yellow blazes and passing five more I-beams on the way.

The bright orange paint blazes that begin south of the county line continue along the path as it ascends the lower slopes of Partlow Mountain. This is basically the Old Red Horse Trail over the mountain to the Robinson River, the Sliding Falls, and beyond; it becomes increasingly hard to follow.

The old Albany Trail does not come in from the southeast to connect with the existing path, but it is known that hunters use remnants of the trail as it goes southeast to Gal Pond, Cracker Pond, and beyond.

63 High Falls and The Plains via High Falls Loop Trail

Trail, hiking, lean-to, camping, swimming, fishing, waterfall
5.9 miles, 3 hours, 320 foot elevation change (west side of loop); 6.5 miles, 3 hours, 300 foot elevation change (east side of loop)
A 0.5-mile spur from either leg of this loop leads to High Falls
Entire route has been remarked in red discs, maps XI, XIII, XIV, and XV

In an effort to eliminate maintenance on problem trails and better manage the trail network near High Falls, the DEC has joined several trails into this loop. It is made up of fragments and rerouted sections of former trails and has just been marked with red discs over its entire length. All other trails and destinations except Darning Needle and Fishpole ponds (section 84) are accessible from this loop, underscoring its strategic importance.

To reach the western end of the loop, drive south across the iron bridge over the Oswegatchie River in Wanakena onto South Shore Road. The road curves left, and as it straightens out, you should look for a road turning off to the right. The trail begins here as signs indicate, but you cannot park here because a nearby residence requires it for access to a driveway. Parking has traditionally been accommodated at a small turnoff about 100 feet farther along South Shore Road, just past a tennis court. The eastern end of the loop similarly begins on an old road leading off to the right, another 0.4 mile down South Shore Road. There is a formal parking area which is scheduled to be enlarged.

The western end of the loop was the beginning of a nine-mile railroad built by the Rich Lumber Company around 1902. It paralleled the Oswegatchie River and ended in the vicinity of The Plains. It was later developed into the High Falls Truck Trail for the purpose of fire protection and management by the state. Though it was used by official vehicles as late as 1983, flooding has always been a problem in the areas where it nears the river and the westernmost 5.7 miles of it has now been abandoned. The first mile of the road is designated the Wanakena Primitive Corridor since the Wanakena Water Company maintains water lines originating at springs one mile up the road.

After passing the residence on the right, you come to a register and a

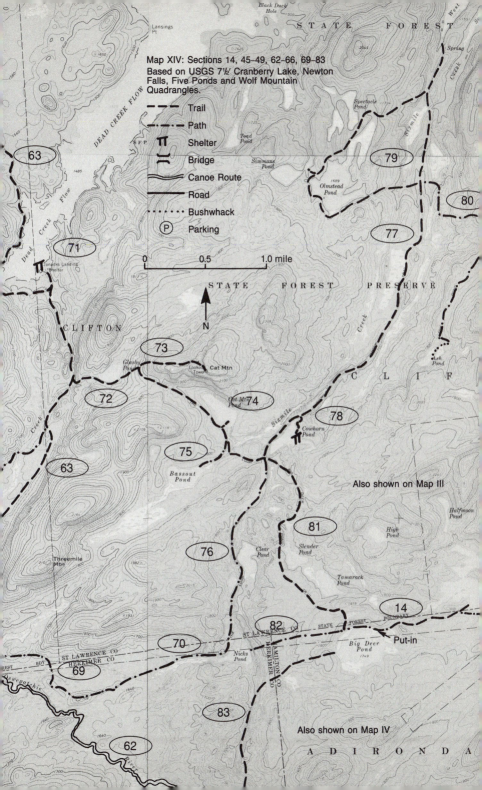

Map XIV: Sections 14, 45–49, 62–66, 69–83
Based on USGS 7½' Cranberry Lake, Newton
Falls, Five Ponds and Wolf Mountain
Quadrangles.

- – – Trail
- · – · Path
- Shelter
- Bridge
- Canoe Route
- Road
- · · · · Bushwhack
- Ⓟ Parking

0   0.5   1.0 mile

STATE   FOREST   PRESERVE

N

Also shown on Map III

Also shown on Map IV

barrier at the beginning of state land. The road passes through a small stand of balsams in five minutes, then crosses Skate Creek over two culverts. The area is frequently flooded for about 15 feet, but the water is not likely to be deep. In under twenty minutes, after entering the mostly hardwood forest, you come to a sizeable stream. Not far beyond, yellow paint blazes indicate the start of the Dobson Trail (section 65), a rough hunters' path that turns left and leads to High Falls. Fifteen minutes later, you will come to a junction at 1.9 miles where maintenance of the High Falls Truck Trail ends. The continuing Truck Trail, which forks right, is described in section 64.

The loop continues over the Leary Trail to the left. This 2.8-mile trail is named after a family who ran a popular hotel in Wanakena. Art Leary also ran a sportsman's camp on the Oswegatchie River below the trail to Five Ponds and this trail provided a more direct approach than the railroad bed. It passes over a series of low hills and has a number of muddy spots due not to beaver flooding, but instead to erosion.

In the first twenty minutes along the Leary Trail, you will climb through a modest draw, dip to an intermittent stream, climb over a small hill and descend to a second, larger stream which you cross below a small beaver pond. You then begin a long, but gradual ascent that should take you up the shoulder of another hill in twenty-five minutes. An easy descent follows through an interesting section of tall hardwoods with an understory of short spruce and balsam. It takes you ten minutes to reach a stream crossing where traces of old logging roads are evident. The trail then swings left and takes you near the edge of an attractive beaver pond with grassy shores. The trail used to cross the pond's outlet and follow the bed of a railroad spur that led south and recrossed the outlet before joining the main railroad in less than half a mile. This route was prone to frequent flooding, so the trail was rerouted and now stays to the west of the outlet. As you cover the last 0.2 mile of the present route of the Leary Trail, you pass through what appears to be a small burned-over area with low bushes, ferns, and tall grass.

The junction with the truck trail is reached two hours and 4.7 miles from the trailhead and the loop continues east from this point. A right turn here will take you 75 feet to a newly cut trail which leads south and in 400 feet connects with the trail to Five Ponds (section 66). The portion of the truck trail visible to the west of this junction is already beginning to fill with blowdown and shows how fast nature begins to reclaim a trail once it is no longer maintained.

High Falls is almost 1.7 miles away. Turn left and you come to the former junction of the Leary Trail after 400 feet. Sixty feet farther is the

Looking northeast across The Plains to Threemile Mountain

junction where the old trail to Five Ponds turns off to the right. The trail ahead is often flooded as it crosses a stream and you must step carefully on the accumulated debris to avoid getting wet feet. After negotiating another wet spot, you emerge from the woods and catch your first sight of the Oswegatchie River. The river is quite narrow here as it winds through spruce, tamarack, and alder thickets. Beyond the large rock outcropping on the left is a designated campsite with an outhouse, picnic table, and room for several tents. This is a popular site for hikers and canoeists and is so heavily used during certain seasons that it may look and smell objectionable.

Glasby Creek flows into the river in this area. Just past Carters Landing, named for Cornelius Carter, a guide who had a camp at the north end of The Plains, you cross Glasby Creek on a plank bridge. The area beyond has usually been flooded over the boot-tops for a distance of 40 feet, but this condition now appears to have been corrected. Once across, you swing right and follow the trail as it rises up to skirt the southern edge of The Plains—a large, open expanse of grassland that extends almost a mile to the northeast. It is unknown whether this was caused by a fire or some phenomenon of geology, but its existence has been artificially extended by people who cut the grass as a source of hay or grazed sheep here in the early part of this century. Five minutes past The Plains, you reach the junction of the Old Plains Trail (section 65), which has been rerouted. The new trail begins at a junction about three minutes farther along the loop and now serves as the eastern side of the High Falls Loop Trail.

The truck trail, the right fork, is now quite enjoyable to walk and as you head south, you will notice a large, tracked vehicle on the right. This vehicle was used to maintain the bed of the road and now rests as a derelict reminder of bygone days. The trail makes a gradual swing to the left around a knoll, but you may notice a path that cuts left and goes over the top of the knoll, passing a campsite before rejoining the trail on the opposite side. The truck trail ends just beyond, at High Falls, although the red-marked trail used to continue from a junction before the lean-to. It went on to Pine Ridge (section 67) and Nicks and Clear ponds (section 76), then ended at the junction southwest of Cowhorn Pond. It is now officially abandoned, but is still used to reach those destinations.

Note that the bridge at High Falls has been removed (although the lean-to and outhouse on the south shore were still there in August 1989), so there is no easy way to connect with the old routes south (see section 62 for more details).

The eastern end of the High Falls Loop Trail begins as previously described along an old road that was also the route of one of the Rich Lumber Company's logging railroads. A barrier stands at the beginning of the trail, but there is no register or destination sign. Following red markers, you hike southeast through tall hardwoods with occasional stands of spruce and balsam in adjacent swampy lowlands. One half hour from the trailhead, the trail dips to a wet area that has at times been flooded up to fifteen inches deep for a distance of 200 feet. A detour leads right on the fill of the former Cucumber Creek rail spur. After the rerouting leaves the fill, the backwaters are already beginning to invade low spots. On the main roadbed, the grades are so easy and the ground so firm that you can cover the nearly 2 miles to Dead Creek Flow in 45 minutes.

The road ends at the edge of the flow, which became a bay of Cranberry Lake when its level was raised. There is a campsite here and a path to the sandy beach beyond. The trail turns right here and becomes a more rugged foot trail headed southwest, then east as it curves around the flow. The planks that bridge several small streams are apt to be very slippery at times. Twenty-five minutes and 1.1 miles from the Dead Creek Flow campsite, you reach a junction where the short (0.2-mile) trail from Janacks Landing (section 71) comes in on the left. Because this is a popular point of access to the trail system for boaters and canoeists, a register is located here, 3.1 miles from the start of your walk.

Oswegatchie River at Carter's Landing on the High Falls Truck Trail

From the register, the trail turns south, passing a small, but dense, evergreen swamp on the left. Following the route of an old logging road, you begin to climb along a stream, encountering a few annoying wet areas as you cross over to the left side, then recross to the right. The grade steepens, but ends abruptly at a junction in a draw twenty-five minutes and 0.8 mile from the register. This is called the Sand Hill Junction and the left fork gives access to the trails and destinations to the east as described later in this chapter. It is 3.9 miles and one hour and thirty-five minutes from the South Shore Road trailhead, or 1 mile and one half hour from Janacks Landing. Your climb from Janacks Landing to the junction covers 160 vertical feet.

To continue on to High Falls, you now bear right and descend into the valley of Glasby Creek. This is the northern end of the former Plains trail. The trail crosses Glasby Creek in less than 0.1 mile, below a pretty waterfall on the left. Leveling off, the trail parallels the creek, with its wetlands visible to the right. After ten minutes, at 4.4 miles, you see the tread of the old Plains trail continuing straight ahead into wet terrain. An arrow directs you to turn left toward drier land along the base of Threemile

Mountain. For the next twenty minutes, you hike through this zone of transition and though it has a few wet areas, any inconvenience is offset by the interesting surroundings. Three small waterfalls at various points tumble down from the mountain's shoulder on the left, their streams disappearing into the dense wetland growth on the right. After leaving the base of the mountain, you soon come to a substantial flooded area which can be crossed on an old beaver dam to the right. As an alternative, a tall tree trunk has been felled to provide a fifty-foot "bridge." Once across, the trail swings left, then makes a wide swing right as it seeks the easiest route through some hillocks. You finally come to the end of the trail, at 6.5 miles, at a junction on the truck trail, 2.1 miles from the Sand Hill Junction, but still 0.5 mile short of High Falls.

The total distance for the complete loop with a visit to High Falls is 12.4 miles and it makes for a full day's hike. You should allow extra time for the mile-long round trip to the falls, for enjoying the many different types of terrain encountered, as well as for negotiating areas of problem flooding.

64　High Rock and Beyond via Abandoned High Falls Truck Trail

Abandoned trail along old railroad bed, camping
5.8 miles, 2¾ hours (between ends of Leary Trail), relatively level, maps XI, XIV, and XV

This section of the High Falls Truck Trail passes some interesting and very scenic areas; and despite its abandonment, hunters have been keeping it fairly free of blowdown. There is little that can be done about the flooding, however, and so this attractive, historic route is unfortunately destined to become a little-used wilderness path. A few red DEC markers remain, but they will soon disappear.

Heading west from the junction of the Leary Trail, you come to a large wetland on the right in fifteen minutes. It is filled with magnificent, tall, dead, standing timber and gives you an immediate feeling of being deep in the wilderness. As you walk along it, look for a very old sign on the right which marks the Albany Road (section 62). This portion of the old road has been opened up through the wetland by hunters and trappers, but a glance to the left, into the woods, shows the current state of most of the road—nonexistent!

Old Bridge over Glasby Creek on the Old Plains Trail

One half hour past the Albany Road, you complete a long, gradual ascent and arrive at a fork in the path with an old fire ring. A right turn will take you to two designated camping sites with an outhouse at High Rock, a rocky bluff on the edge of the Oswegatchie River, just over 0.1 mile away. This is 2.3 miles from the Leary Trail junction, or 4.2 miles from Wanakena. The old truck trail swings left at the fork and descends to cross a stream on a concrete bridge in under ten minutes. The stream emerges from the woods on the left, sliding gracefully down rock slabs to the bridge, then flattens out as it enters the Oswegatchie wetlands.

As you continue along the path of the truck trail, notice how it follows a division in the tree growth. To your right, balsam, spruce, and tamarack thrive in the wet river lowlands, while on the higher ground to the left, the forest is dominated by hardwoods and an occasional hemlock. One half hour past High Rock, a major flooded area is likely to give you great difficulty, if not wet feet. The path may be flooded for a distance of up to 200 feet and your best passage is on the right over a low, muddy beaver dam.

The path soon makes a broad swing to the left and less than ten minutes past the flooded area, you come to a small clearing on the left, 2 miles from High Rock, 6.2 from Wanakena. On the right, you may see an old signpost lying in the bushes. The old trail to Cage Lake Springhole, Buck Pond, and Cage Lake started here, but since its abandonment, it is rapidly fading.

Without the bridge, there is no easy crossing of the river except to wade or swim.

Beyond this former junction, the path passes an old gravel pit and continues on to meet the river at Ross Rapids and again at Straight Rapids. The new junction of the blue-marked trail to Five Ponds is at 5.8 miles, 7.7 miles from Wanakena. The new junction with the south end of the Leary Trail is 75 feet ahead.

65 Dobson Trail and Old Plains Trail
Hunters' path, abandoned trail, maps XI, XIII, XIV, and XV

Bert Dobson knew that his clients would not want to waste any time getting to his camp at High Falls, so he cut a bee-line trail that endures to this day. Though not an official trail, hunters maintain most of it to a passable degree so, in keeping with this guide's format, it will be referred to as a path. It is steeper than the Leary Trail, which parallels it to the west, but much drier. Its 3-mile length could be developed into a desirable route for the hiking public, but for now it exists with sporadic marking, vagueness at its southern end, and a terminus on the now abandoned Plains Trail. The Plains Trail was recently abandoned because of flooding at its Glasby Creek crossings.

From its beginning on the High Falls Truck Trail (section 63), the Dobson Trail steadily ascends, following mostly yellow paint blazes and a well-defined foot tread. A few level stretches give you a chance to take a break and enjoy the tall hardwood forest along the way. In twenty minutes, you reach the top of a hill, after which the path drops steeply to a very wet clearing. Blazes seem to stop, though the way is sometimes flagged with tape, another questionable practice that frequently litters the woods. You should proceed along the right edge of the clearing, picking up the foot tread after about 150 feet to follow it through another wet spot.

The path now becomes a bit rougher as you dip to cross Dead Creek on rocks. Climbing away from the creek, the path follows up the rocky cut of a seasonal rivulet. After ten minutes you arrive at the top of another hill, northeast of Roundtop Mountain. A steady descent now begins that will take you down through open hardwood slopes where many springs originate. The descent lessens after fifteen minutes and the path becomes very hard to see. Some inconsiderate woodsman has recently left large axe blazes in several trees in an attempt to mark the last stretch of the path.

This ignorant practice not only causes unsightly, irreversible damage to the trees, it is also illegal. By following this ugly course, you should reach the old Plains Trail in 0.3 mile.

The old Plains Trail can be picked up from the eastern half of the High Falls Loop Trail, about 0.7 mile southwest of Sand Hill Junction. Here, an arrow points left to keep you on the loop, but the tread of the old trail, which continues 1.8 miles to the truck trail, is seen ahead. It gets very wet as it approaches wetlands along Glasby Creek, which it crosses on a deteriorating wooden walkway. Once on the northwestern side of the creek, it rises slightly above the wetlands, but muddy spots are still a problem. After crossing a stream draining down from Roundtop Mountain, you reach the area where the Dobson Trail enters on the right. A second crossing of Glasby Creek could still be made on a rickety plank walkway in 1989, but it is just a matter of time before it rots away and you will have to cross on a beaver dam 75 feet downstream. Between the walkway and the dam, the beaver flow submerged the once famous "Boiling Spring."

The southern 0.5 mile of the trail is relatively dry and it makes a good side trip from the High Falls Truck Trail. It crosses The Plains and is therefore the best way to see and study them. Note the white pines of varying ages and size that contrast with the surrounding grasses and brush, making this a truly unique area.

66 Five Ponds

Trail, hiking, lean-tos, camping, fishing, moderate grades
2.1 miles, 1⅓ hours (from High Falls Loop Trail to first lean-to); 2.7 miles, 1⅔ hours (from High Falls Loop Trail to second lean-to), maps XIV and XV

Taken separately, there is nothing unique or distinguished about Little Five, Big Five, Little Shallow, Big Shallow, and Washbowl—the Five Ponds. As wilderness ponds go, they are as unassuming as most other obscure bodies of water are and rather plain. It is the origin and orientation of this cluster, however, that is significant. Their depressions were likely formed by the melting of blocks of ice from the last glaciation, 10,000 years ago. That same glacier left a long, sinuous esker in its wake that separated Little Five and Big Five from the other three. It has long been regarded as one of the classic Adirondack eskers and rises to a maximum height of 150 feet. A study of the 7.5-minute Five Ponds and

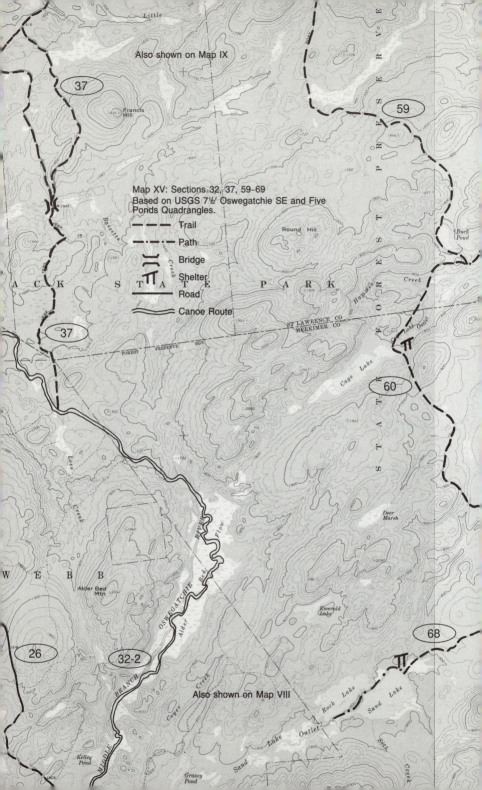

Also shown on Map IX

Map XV: Sections 32, 37, 59-69
Based on USGS 7½' Oswegatchie SE and Five
Ponds Quadrangles.

——— Trail
—··— Path
      Bridge
      Shelter
——— Road
      Canoe Route

Also shown on Map VIII

Also shown on Map XI and Map XIV

Little Shallow Pond

Oswegatchie SE topographic maps shows that this same esker extends, albeit interrupted, for at least 6 miles, past Wolf Pond to Sand and Rock lakes (section 68), which it also separates.

From the new junction on the High Falls Loop Trail (section 63), the trail follows blue markers down to a beaver-flooded area, which it crosses uneasily on a muddy dam. Just before the crossing, you may notice a path continuing on along the north side of the flooded area. This is the former route of the trail; it leads 0.1 mile to the old junction on the High Falls Truck Trail.

In five minutes, you cross the Oswegatchie River on a wide, wooden bridge that is in very good shape. A designated campsite is just ahead and another is to the left, but both are heavily used and can be quite unpleasant. A dense spruce and balsam forest lines the trail and in under ten minutes, you come to a junction where an unmarked path turns right. It leads to campsites along the river near the spot where Art Leary had his camp. Wolf Pond Outlet, which also carries the combined outlets of the Five Ponds, meets the river here. You should turn left at the junction and follow the blue-marked trail as it works its way over to parallel wetlands along the Wolf Pond Outlet on the right. As is to be expected, there are numerous wet spots, including three stream crossings. After forty minutes, at 1.2 miles, the trail swings away from the wetland and heads over to the stream that drains the waters to the east of the esker. You will enjoy the ascent through the mixed woods along this section because it is drier and quite pretty. After crossing the stream on rocks, a wetland forms alongside it on the left.

Shortly, you cross the Totten and Crossfield line into Herkimer County with its virgin forests. The high rib of land on your right is the beginning of the esker and you will follow the trail along its base to Big Shallow Pond, twenty minutes away. The lean-to there has a dirt floor, but is in fairly good condition. It faces up the pond and there are rocks on the shore nearby from which to wade or fish. The outhouse is in good shape and sits off to the right of the lean-to, at the base of the esker.

A well-defined path to the left of the outhouse leads steeply up to the top of the esker, 0.1 mile away, in ten minutes. Heading over to the west side of the esker, you should be able to see a path leading southwest. It takes you to a steep descent to Big Five Pond near its outlet, five minutes and 0.2 mile away. You may find a canoe here and the view up the pond toward Panther Mountain is scenic. It is a bit harder to find the path heading 0.2 mile north to Little Five Pond, but it does exist. The descent is just as steep and much more dense. Other paths exist along the esker, including one that continues southwest along its top, dropping down to cross an inlet to Little Shallow Pond. They can, however, be confusing and annoying with blowdown; so be careful should you attempt to follow them. Though white pines are the trees usually associated with eskers, hemlock is the dominant species in this area.

To reach Washbowl and Little Shallow ponds, follow the trail as it crosses the outlet of Big Shallow Pond on rocks, 100 feet before the lean-to. It rises slightly as it skirts a wetland on the left. After crossing the tiny outlet of Washbowl Pond, you climb gradually along a knoll from which you can see Washbowl Pond down through the trees to the left. Swinging left, then right, you descend along the trail to the lean-to at Little Shallow Pond. Its outhouse is behind to the left, and both facilities are in the same condition as the ones at Big Shallow Pond. A path in front leads to the brushy, log-lined edge of the pond.

67 Wolf Pond from Five Ponds

Trail, hiking, lean-to, camping, easy grades
2.1 miles, 1¼ hours (from Little Shallow Pond lean-to); 4.8
miles, 3 hours (from High Falls Loop Trail), map XV

If you continue southwest along the blue-marked trail past Five Ponds, you quickly come to a dismal-looking swamp along an inlet to Little Shallow Pond. You must cross it in an area of wet blowdown that requires coordination if you want to keep your feet dry. Once across, you follow along the base of the esker with the swamp close by on the left. Gaining elevation, you leave the wetland behind, following the narrow stream that feeds it. You cross, then recross that stream as you ascend. The remainder of the trail is relatively dry and after forty-five minutes, the esker diminishes to the point of being undiscernible. Mature hardwoods are more prevalent with spruce, balsam, and hemlock mixed in to a lesser degree. After one hour and fifteen minutes, you will reach a junction where the yellow-marked trail from Wolf Pond and Cage Lake comes in on the right. Ten minutes down this trail is the Wolf Pond lean-to and other possible campsites described in section 61.

68 Sand Lake and Rock Lake

Trail, hiking, lean-to, camping, fishing, swimming, easy grades
2.3 miles, 1 hour (from Wolf Pond trail junction); 7.1 miles, 4
hours (from High Falls Loop Trail); 11.8 miles, 6½ hours (from
Wanakena), map XV

Sand Lake is the most remote destination in the Five Ponds Wilderness reached by a trail. With its lean-to and 300-foot-long sandy beach, it has long been regarded as the jewel of the area. Its waters drain west into the Middle Branch of the Oswegatchie River as do the waters of Rock Lake, which is separated from Sand Lake by a narrow esker to the west.

To reach these lakes, continue straight ahead on the blue trail past the junction with the Wolf Pond trail. It descends to cross a stream on rocks at the top of a waterfall where the stream tumbles down through a rocky cut on the right. This is a pretty spot and you are likely to hear the water before you see it. After climbing up a short pitch past the stream, the trail

Beach at Sand Lake

moderates and you can occasionally see Wolf Pond through the trees to the right. Small streams and wet spots are minor impediments as the trail moderates and becomes largely uneventful. Just over an hour from the junction, Sand Lake appears ahead. The lean-to is to the right, just before the woods gives way to the beach. It has a dirt floor and is in good shape. Its outhouse is fair and located to the rear.

Look for a path near the north end of the beach; you can follow it up onto the low esker that separates Sand Lake from Rock Lake. Heading southwest along the esker, you come to a narrow section in fifteen minutes where Rock Lake rests in isolation, barely 30 feet from Sand Lake. The path continues along the esker to another narrow section, fifteen minutes further.

Take time to explore the ponds, the esker, and the outlet of Sand Lake, and contemplate Verplanck Colvin's first visit to the ponds. In 1878, he resurveyed the boundary of Brown's Tract and the Totten and Crossfield Purchase, which was originally surveyed in 1772 by Archibald Campbell. The survey line crosses the outlet of Sand Lake. When Colvin visited the lakes (he called Rock Lake "Wolf Lake"), he found the same open walking along the esker that you will find today, but the head of Rock Lake was tangled with fallen timber. In wading along the north shore to circle the lake, he fell into "a cold, heavy quicksand and descended so suddenly that I barely had time to grasp some laurel bushes at the shore, and with difficulty escaped entire submergence and drowning."

69 Pine Ridge

Path along abandoned trail, camping, moderate grades
1.3 miles, 50 minutes (from High Falls), maps XIII, XIV, and XV

Pine Ridge was always renowned for its majestic stands of old growth white pines, but many were toppled during the Big Blow of 1950. The ones remaining are still an impressive sight, but reaching them has been made more difficult since the trail between High Falls and Cowhorn Junction was officially abandoned due to chronic flooding. The trail west of Nicks Pond now has several troublesome wet areas and stream crossings that must be negotiated on a trip to Pine Ridge. The red markers have been removed, but the route is still visible as a path.

From the former junction at High Falls, the path heads east through a mixed woods. There are frequent blowdowns and muddy spots and you have to find rocks or logs to cross several small streams if it has been very wet. After a half hour, you come to the Nicks Pond outlet, which is just wide enough that you can't jump across and just deep enough that you don't want to wade. Currently, a log downstream is your best option, though it may wash out in times of flooding. Ahead of you, the land rises and the contour of a pine-topped esker stands out. This is Pine Ridge and the path climbs steeply straight up to its crest. A short bushwhack either way along the esker will take you to remaining stands of the trees.

While on the ridge, look for a yellow-blazed path forking off to the right. It drops down to cross a wet area, then enters a dense stand of trees on the bank of the Oswegatchie River. Camp Johnny, a small clearing on the bank, stood here, 150 yards from the former trail. This is a popular, and therefore overused, campsite that allows canoeists access to Pine Ridge.

70   Nicks Pond from the West
Path along abandoned trail, camping, easy grades
2.9 miles, 1½ hours (from High Falls), maps III, XIII, and XIV

The former trail continues east as a path from Pine Ridge to Nicks Pond. It is extremely rough and penetrates a ruggedly beautiful section of the wilderness. Descending from the esker, you enter a spruce and balsam bog with frequent muddy spots. Thirty minutes after you leave Pine Ridge, you recross Nicks Pond outlet on thin logs. As you approach Nicks Pond, the path swings north, rising 75 feet above the level of the pond. A campsite lies along the path within sight of the pond and a short bushwhack will take you down to its brushy edge. From the campsite, the path continues north to Clear Pond (section 76).

71   Janacks Landing
Canoe access to trails, lean-to, camping, swimming, maps XI, XIII, and XIV

This point of access to the trail system is located near the extreme south end of Dead Creek Flow, along the eastern shore. It is frequently used by

Looking east across Glasby Pond toward Cat Mountain

canoeists as well as power boaters and can be quite congested during the summer months. The lean-to and outhouse are in fairly good condition and there are other campsites nearby. A path leads 150 feet to the sandy beach and a trail with yellow DEC markers heads south from the lean-to and connects with the High Falls Loop Trail, 0.2 mile away (section 63). As of 1988, this short trail was in poor condition from blowdown, flooding, and lack of markers. The landing is named after John Janack, who manned the tower for its first 23 years and lived with his wife and eleven children in a cabin at the landing.

72 Glasby Pond

Trail, hiking, campsite, fishing
0.3 mile, 10 minutes, 100-foot vertical rise from Sand Hill Junction, maps XIII and XIV

From Sand Hill Junction, a trail heads east for 2.3 miles to Cowhorn Junction, the hub of trails in the eastern sector of the network. It has been remarked with yellow DEC markers, replacing the red ones that might have caused confusion with the High Falls Loop Trail. Glasby Pond, named for Nick Glasby, another legendary hunter and trapper, is the first feature along this trail.

From Sand Hill Junction, the trail climbs along the slope of a steep hill, then makes a sharp left turn and parallels Glasby Creek to your right. An easy bushwhack over to the creek will take you to a small waterfall less than 100 feet away. The grade eases up and you come to a clearing where several pieces of hardware left from logging operations can be found poking up through the ferns and grass. Leaving the clearing, you continue straight ahead to the outlet of Glasby Pond, where there is a nice view of Cat Mountain rising up in the distance. A beaver dam to your right spans the outlet and the trail crosses just below it on a series of logs. There is a small campsite 100 feet farther along on the opposite side and a path along the brushy shore.

73   Cat Mountain

Trail, hiking, camping, views
1.4 miles, ¾ hour, 600-foot vertical rise from Sand Hill Junction, maps XIII and XIV

According to Bob Marshall, George and John Muir's father was out checking his trap lines when he saw a wildcat on a ledge on this mountain, hence its name. One of the first fire towers in the state was erected on the summit of Cat Mountain in 1909. It was a wooden structure placed there after fires had become a problem in that area, as well as the rest of the Adirondacks, during the previous decade. It was later replaced by a steel tower and although that one was removed over a decade ago, you can still enjoy views to the west and south from open ledges.

Continuing along the yellow-marked trail past the campsite at Glasby Pond (section 72), you climb a knoll on the pond's southern edge. Upon descending you come to an extremely muddy section that lasts for the next 0.1 mile until the trail begins to ascend away from the pond. Steady, moderate climbing takes you to a junction at the 0.7-mile point where the poorly marked trail to Cowhorn Junction turns right. You continue straight ahead, now following red markers that denote the spur trail to Cat Mountain.

Climbing eases up in the next ten minutes as you follow contours along the north slope of the mountain, passing a false summit to the south. A short climb takes you to flat area where you see the cornerstones of the fire observer's cabin off to the left. Across the flat area is a vertical rock wall below the summit and you must follow the trail over to its right side where climbing is possible, but steep! You climb at least eighty feet in elevation before the grade eases and you will have to use your hands in some places.

(Snow and ice accumulation may prohibit winter passage.) Once on top, the trail turns right and rises easily to the exposed rock ledges on the southwest side of the summit where the abutments of the tower remain.

Waves of low, rolling hills spread out before you with Roundtop Mountain to the east and Threemile Mountain to the southeast. Cat Mountain Pond lies directly below you to the south with Mount Electra above it on the horizon. By walking around on the ledges to the south, you can extend your view to include the distant volcano-like cone of Blue Mountain in the southeast. Closer in, about a mile away, you may notice a concentration of pine, spruce, and hemlock contrasting with the surrounding hardwood forest. They mark the location of the esker where the Cowhorn Junction lies. At the extreme eastern edge of the ledges, you can see the Santanoni Range with its long narrow slide.

74 Cat Mountain Pond and Cowhorn Junction

Trail, hiking, campsites, fishing
1.6 miles, ¾ hour from Sand Hill Junction, moderate grades;
2.3 miles, 1¼ hours between Sand Hill Junction and Cowhorn
Junction, maps III, XIII, and XIV

A right turn at the junction with the Cat Mountain Trail (section 74) will take you over a well-defined, but poorly marked and maintained, trail. The markers, when they do appear, are yellow and you follow them the rest of the way to Cowhorn Junction. Swinging southeast, you contour around the western shoulder of Cat Mountain, then begin a moderate descent through a boulder-filled gully. The trail is frequently wet as water drains down it in several places toward Cat Mountain Pond. As the trail levels out, you can see the pond through the trees to the left with the magnificent cliffs of Cat Mountain rising directly behind it. The edges of the pond are brushy with sheep laurel and leatherleaf, and in the spring the blooming witchhopple at the pond's west end is said to be remarkable. The trail crosses a major inlet with several old beaver dams near the south end of the pond. A faint path turns left 100 feet past the inlet and leads 250 feet to a campsite on the shore. Another campsite is to the right, near the outlet. You may see the depression of an old foundation as you explore this area. The Indian Mountain Club used to maintain several camps in this region, one of which was here. Guides from the club would take guests to the camps on hunting and fishing trips during the early 1900s.

Cat Mountain Pond with Cat Mountain Cliffs

As you leave Cat Mountain Pond, the trail rises over a slight knoll, where the path to Bassout Pond (section 75) forks right. The trail then drops to cross the rock-filled outlet of Bassout Pond. It soon becomes very wet where water flows through its depression for about 500 feet. You reach the foot of the esker 0.3 mile from the outlet and a steep forty-foot climb takes you to the Cowhorn Junction on its crest. To the left, the Sixmile Creek Trail (section 77) heads north; while the trails to Clear and Nicks ponds (section 76) and Grassy, Slender, and Big Deer ponds (section 81) diverge from a junction 75 feet to the south.

75 Bassout Pond

Path, campsite, fishing
0.3 mile, 10 minutes, relatively level, maps XIII and XIV

John Bassout, a mid-nineteenth century trapper and hunter, had a camp on the trail from Cat Mountain to Cowhorn Pond. The path to his namesake pond forks right from the yellow-marked trail (section 74) at the high point on the knoll, 150 feet before the crossing of the Bassout Pond outlet. It is now a rough hunters' path that heads southwest, passing a clearing on the left in five minutes. Two minutes later, you will come to a campsite, after which the path is hard to trace and you will end up bushwhacking to reach the pond. Its brushy shores are occasionally interrupted by boulders, while tall spruce and white pines rise overhead. The winter hiker may wish to explore this sizeable pond further as well as the lesser ponds in the extensive wetland to the west.

76 Clear Pond and Nicks Pond

Trail and path, hiking, camping, easy to moderate grades
1.1 miles, 25 minutes (Cowhorn Junction to Clear Pond); 0.6 mile, 15 minutes (Clear Pond to Nicks Pond), maps III, XIII, and XIV

The former red-marked trail to High Falls from Cowhorn Junction has been remarked with blue markers as far south as Clear Pond. Beyond that point, markers have been removed and the trail has been abandoned. From Cowhorn Junction, turn south and follow the trail to a second junction 75 feet away. The yellow marked trail to the left leads to Slender and Big Deer ponds (section 81). Go straight ahead, following blue markers along the crest of the esker. Soon you will drop down the right side of the esker and descend through a draw dominated by hardwoods. The trail levels briefly, then descends again, taking you past a stagnant pool on the right. Clear Pond is just ahead and the trail officially ends here at a small campsite.

It is possible to follow the abandoned section of trail beyond as a path to Nicks Pond. This approach is more desirable than the one described in section 70, because it is drier and much shorter. The forest consists mostly of maple, ash, and yellow birch, with occasional spruce and balsam thickets.

Head south from Clear Pond, paralleling its multi-dammed outlet which is visible in five minutes from a small clearing on the left. You reach another clearing, this one with a campsite, after you climb over a steep knoll. Nicks Pond is less than five minutes ahead. It was named for the trapper Nick Glasby, for whom three of the region's ponds were named. According to Bob Marshall, it was as delightful a body of water as could be imagined. Marshall visited it on a weekend when he scouted out the Hamilton, Herkimer, St. Lawrence county corner, which is a short bushwhack to the northeast.

77 Sixmile Creek Trail and Sliding Rock Falls

Scenic trail, hiking, canoe access, swimming
4.3 miles, 2 hours, 320-foot elevation change, maps III, XI,
XIII, and XIV

This blue-marked trail between Cowhorn Junction and West Flow on Cranberry Lake provides one of the most scenic hikes in the region. Following the route of an esker most of the way, it winds through attractive second-growth forests of spruce, hemlock, maple, beech, and yellow birch. White pines, which are usually found on the sandy ribs of eskers, are, however, conspicuously few in number.

Heading north from the Cowhorn Junction, you catch glimpses of Cowhorn Pond (section 78) down through the trees to your right. In 0.5 mile, you reach a junction where the yellow-marked side trail to its lean-to turns right. For the next twenty-five minutes, you enjoy the elevated terrain with occasional views of wetlands down to the right. After 1.9 miles the esker declines and you bear left, skirting the edge of a wetland. The trail is hard to follow here due to blowdown and infrequent markers; but if you stay back from the edge of the wetland where walking is easier, you should be able locate it. Near the north end of the wetland, the trail swings right and pitches up and over the esker, which is now quite low. Swinging left on the other side, you continue north on drier ground, coming to a junction at almost 3 miles, one hour and ten minutes from Cowhorn Junction. The southern end of the yellow-marked loop trail to Olmstead, Simmons, and Spectacle ponds (section 79) turns left here. To the right is the abandoned trail to Ash Pond (section 80).

Gentle grades take you in fifteen minutes to the crossing of Sixmile Creek at 3.7 miles. To the left, the creek emerges from a wetland and drops about fifteen feet over the wide, sloped rock of Sliding Rock Falls. Just over five minutes past the falls, at 3.9 miles, you will come to a register, placed here for those entering the woods from Cranberry Lake, 0.4 mile to the north. An unmarked path forks off to the right, crosses Sixmile Creek and follows the edge of South Flow to private land at Chair Rock Point. Continuing ahead, you reach the north end of the previously mentioned loop trail 500 feet from the register.

The Sixmile Creek Trail ends ingloriously in an extremely wet descent to the edge of West Flow. It is best to stay to the right since this will take you to a campsite and rocky landing on the right edge of the flow where the trail officially ends.

Old Beaver Dam on Nicks Pond Outlet

8 Cowhorn Pond

Trail, hiking, fishing, lean-to, camping, swimming
0.2-mile spur trail, maps III, XIII, and XIV

Leaving the Sixmile Creek Trail 0.5 mile north of Cowhorn Junction, the yellow-marked side trail to the Cowhorn Pond Lean-to drops off the east side of the esker, curves right around a swampy bay, and ends 0.2 mile later at a point on the eastern shore. The lean-to has a dirt floor and is in poor condition, as is the outhouse. Due to the fact that it is relatively easy to reach from Cranberry Lake, it is heavily used and therefore quite littered. This is unfortunate, especially since this pond is attractively situated in a steep-walled basin clothed in a maturing mixed woods. A campsite is located directly south across the pond, but it is not easy to reach. The pond is shaped like a cowhorn, hence its name.

9 Olmstead, Simmons, and Spectacle Ponds

Loop trail, hiking, fishing, lean-to, camping, swimming
2.9 miles, 1¾ hours, moderate grades, maps III, XI, XIII, and XIV

Simmons and Olmstead were both post–Civil War trappers. Indeed, it seems as if every hunter or trapper who ventured into the region is immortalized with his own pond.

This trail originally ended at the Olmstead Pond Lean-to, but was extended along existing informal fishermen's paths in 1988. It has several wet sections where poor drainage and soft ground have turned it into muddy quagmires. From the junction on the Sixmile Creek Trail, 3 miles north of Cowhorn Junction, the yellow-marked trail heads west, descending to cross Sixmile Creek on a plank bridge at 0.2 mile. From here, it begins an ascent of 120 feet along the outlet of Olmstead Pond. At 0.6 mile, it crosses the outlet on rocks and logs just below a beaver dam at the pond's edge. As you work your way counterclockwise around the south side of the pond, the trail rises along the shoulder of a hill, then drops to reach the lean-to after a half hour, at 1.1 miles. It is in good shape, but has a dirt floor and is very littered, like the Cowhorn Pond Lean-to. Behind it, a path leads to a good outhouse; in front, another path leads 175 feet out onto a brushy point at the water's edge.

Sliding Rock Falls on Sixmile Creek Trail

The trail continues around the pond, never far from its edge, and at 1.4 miles, a side trail turns left. It also has yellow markers and leads 0.1 mile to the brushy edge of a small extension of Simmons Pond. The main trail swings back to Olmstead Pond where it passes through two campsites along the northwest shore. The second site has an especially nice rock slab from which to swim or fish.

Climbing away from Olmstead Pond for fifteen minutes, you reach a high overlook above Spectacle Pond at 2 miles. From here, you look down the length of the pond, but use care; the drop is at least fifty feet and the growth underfoot can be slippery. The trail descends to the east where a side trail forks left to the brushy shore of the pond 100 feet away. Leaving the pond, you come to a wet area in five minutes where the trail crosses below an old beaver dam on the left. You soon begin to lose elevation as the trail begins a steady, wet descent that ends in fifteen minutes at a stream crossing. A short pitch ahead takes you up to the Sixmile Creek Trail at a point 0.9 mile north of the junction where you began.

80 Ash Pond

Path
2.2 miles, 1¼ hours, 280-foot vertical rise, maps III, XIII, and XIV

The trail to Ash Pond is now officially abandoned, but the tread is fairly visible and there are occasional markers to look for should you decide to try to follow it. It leaves the Sixmile Creek Trail directly across from the junction of the southern end of the yellow-marked loop trail, 3 miles north of Cowhorn Junction. Descending from the junction, you cross the Cowhorn Pond outlet at 0.1 mile. A steady series of moderate ascents takes you south, then east as you work your way up the ridge south of Indian Mountain. After a half hour, the trail swings south and the grade eases, but blowdown frequently makes the going rough. The second-growth forest has grown tall and the feeling of wilderness is great. After one hour of not-so-easy hiking, you come to a clearing where there is a heavily littered campsite. If markers exist beyond this point, they are hard to see. Paths go farther, but are unreliable. To find Ash Pond, follow the stream on the south edge of the clearing. It flows west through a swamp and reaches the tiny pond in another 0.1 mile. Like so many other obscure ponds, this one has brush-lined shores and is slowly filling in with vegetation. It has a natural rock-dammed outlet whose stream tumbles 150 feet to the base of the Sixmile Creek Trail esker, one half mile to the west.

Simmons Pond

81 Grassy, Slender, and Big Deer Ponds

Trail, hiking, camping
2.2 miles, 1 hour, easy to moderate grades, maps III, XIII, and XIV

The yellow-marked trail to these ponds heads south, then west from Cowhorn Junction through a mixed woods where you will find some small clearings near a stream after a ten-minute walk. The remains of a foundation are in one of these clearings on the left. Grassy Pond is just past the clearings and a path leads 25 feet to its edge. Swing south again, climb high and away from Grassy Pond, and you approach Slender Pond. Its boggy outline can be seen below to the left through the trees.

Another twenty-five minutes of rolling trail ends in a descent that takes you to a junction within sight of Big Deer Pond. Trail markers end here and a right turn takes you over a path heading west toward Nicks Pond (section 82). Turn left here and proceed along a well-defined route along the north edge of Big Deer Pond that leads in five minutes to a campsite. This is the end of the canoe carry from Lows Lake (section 14).

82 Nicks Pond from Big Deer Pond

Hunters' path, maps III, XIII, and XIV

From the junction at Big Deer Pond where the yellow-marked trail from Cowhorn Junction ends, this path heads west, roughly following the St. Lawrence County line. It is quite rough in some areas and can be difficult to see in many places throughout its 1-mile length. There are several moderate grades and the last 0.3 mile is very tiring as you drop steeply to cross the outlet of Big Deer Pond only to climb over a steep esker on the opposite side. Though it does provide a significant shortcut to Nicks Pond, this route is best left to experienced wilderness navigators.

83 Canoe Carry Between Big Deer Pond and the Oswegatchie River

Canoe carry trail, camping
1.9 miles, 1 hour 10 minutes, moderate grades, maps III, IV, XIII, and XIV

At first glance, this carry seems to be more effort than it is worth, and indeed, it is long as carries go. Though it is wide and well-marked with yellow canoe carry markers, it is still too rough for wheeled carriers, and for those who cannot shuttle all their gear in one trip, it begins to look like a forbidding trek. A second look, however, shows that it is a relatively short carry for one that spans two watersheds, follows such historic routes, and offers such a long through paddle. And, except for the 600-foot carry around Lows Upper dam and the carry to Big Deer Pond, it is the only overland carry on the entire Bog River–Oswegatchie River canoe route. Also, once you reach the Oswegatchie River, it's all downstream from there. While it may not be on every canoeist's list of things to do, it is better that it exists for that smaller number of people who want to do it than not to exist at all. If you are prepared for a true carry of that length, the complete trip will provide you with ample rewards and fond memories.

Big Deer Pond was originally known as Colvin's "Lost Pond," because the country surrounding it is very flat and without landmarks. Indeed, without the new trail, you might find yourself lost while hiking off designated routes in this area. After carrying to Big Deer Pond (section 14), paddle across to its southwest corner, where this carry begins.

You head west-southwest from the take-out point as you climb over a small hill. A small beaver-flooded area appears in fifteen minutes and you must bear right to cross it on an old dam. The carry resumes on the opposite side of the flooded area and begins a gradual climb up through a draw. After twenty more minutes, you reach a height-of-land where there are two split log benches to rest on. This is roughly the halfway point.

From the rest stop, the carry descends into a long depression where the forest is noticeably open. Rolling contours take you in stages to the put-in on the Oswegatchie River near the area long known as Beaverdam. There is a campsite here and a spring flowing out from under the riverbank to the left. A sign marks the beginning of the carry for those few who approach it from the west.

84. Darning Needle and Fishpole Ponds

Trail accessible by canoe, hiking, camping, fishing
2.4 miles, 1¼ hours, easy grades, maps III and XIII

The trail to Darning Needle Pond begins at the extreme upper end of Chair Rock Flow on the southeastern corner of Cranberry Lake. A sign at a campsite marks the start of the trail that bears right, taking you through a handsome mixed woods along an old logging road. After paralleling Chair Rock Creek on your right for fifteen minutes, the road heads straight to the creek bank and the trail turns left. The creek was named for a rock formation on an island at the mouth of the creek.

The trail now becomes very rough and is in need of clearing, but there are usually enough markers to guide you along. A short climb brings you to a campsite near a wetland along the creek at 0.7 mile.

You now head east, away from the creek, then gradually swing back to the south. Except for a few small stream crossings, the next mile is uneventful, but changing trail conditions keep you alert. If you do lose your way, stay near the creek; the trail is never far from it. After one and one half hours, you come to a wetland at 1.5 miles. Markers lead you straight to the edge then stop, and the best way to get across is to go 50 feet to the right where there is a sturdy beaver dam. On the opposite side, markers resume and you turn left, following them along an interesting rocky rib that forms a natural barrier, creating the wetland beyond. After crossing Chair Rock Creek, you make a gradual swing to the southeast, staying well back from the water. Young saplings and viburnums make the

Darning Needle Pond, Graves Mountain in distance

trail obscure in some areas, but you should reach the south end of Darning Needle Pond a half hour past the rib. The woods is open enough to allow some limited camping, but the shoreline is mostly brushy.

There is a proposal to build a nearly mile-long trail southwest from the rocky rib to Fishpole Pond, another favorite wilderness fishing hole, but it will probably not happen until more urgent maintenance issues in the unit are taken care of. The 15-minute Cranberry Lake topographic map (1921) show several trails in this region, one heading south through the draw west of Wolf Mountain. Such a trail would provide access to Grass Pond, now a bay of Lows Lake.

Bob Marshall wrote of walking one of the maze of logging roads from Darning Needle Pond to Little Fish Pond, which he described as "one of the ugliest bodies it has ever been my misfortune to see." He followed routes south over burned-over hills to Graves Mountain, but these routes remain on private land. With classmates, he used these routes to reach Grass Pond Mountain, where the students marked a trail (see section 13).

Scattered Northern Parcels

CURRENTLY, THERE ARE approximately 10,000 acres of isolated, somewhat disjunct parcels of Forest Preserve in the northwest quadrant of the Adirondacks. These parcels and adjoining timber company lands contain some of the finest open peatlands and conifer forests in the entire park and are collectively known as the lower elevation boreal biome. The state is negotiating to consolidate and increase the amount of protected land in this area, so many additional recreational opportunities may be available in the future. During 1988, the state added about 20,000 acres of boreal forest land to these parcels. Tracts have been obtained by both fee and easement and will be open to the public in varying ways at future dates. The following seven chapters contain only hints of how recreational opportunities will be extended to these new lands, all of which are valuable as protection for environmentally and ecologically sensitive areas.

The Yorkshire Tract

As this guide goes to press, the state is completing an easement agreement that gives it development and recreation rights on 19,000 acres owned by the Yorkshire Timber Company. This parcel includes the headwaters of the South Branch of the Grass River and stretches from the Cranberry Lake Wild Forest east to the Horseshoe Lake Wild Forest. It excludes only private lands around Arab Lake and Conifer. The entire tract will be open to the public except for some portions that are being actively logged and except during hunting season (October 20 to December 31). The reservation on hunting rights will expire in fifteen years.

Many logging roads within the tract will be open to the public. Until alternate access points are opened, the public can enter the Yorkshire Tract via the town road through the Massawepie Tract. Details of the recreational potential of the tract will be included in future revisions of this guide, but you are invited to begin discovering this most recent easement acquisition.

Map XVI: Sections 85, 86
Based on NY State DOT 7½' Long Tom
Mountain and USGS 7½' Childwold
Quadrangles.

- - - Trail
———— Road
Ⓟ Parking

Restricted

Catamount
Pond

Restricted

86

Boat Launch

Round
Pond

Long Pond

Pine
Pond

Massawepie Lake

Massawepie Lake

Grass River
Flow

Hardwood
Island

Bootfree
Pond

85

Burnt
Rock

Restricted

Deer
Pond

Town
Line
Pond

1685

Grasse River
Club

OLD RAILROAD GRADE

N

Roaring
Branch

Burntbridge
Pond

Public Access
to Yorkshire Tract

0   0.5   1.0 miles

YORKSHIRE TRACT

Douglas
Rock

2133

Wheeler
Mtn

Massawepie

THIRTY-SIX HUNDRED ACRES of the total forty-five hundred that comprise the Massawepie Tract are currently open for public recreation through a cooperative Fish and Wildlife Management Act (FWMA) agreement between the DEC and the Otetiana Council of the Boy Scouts of America. The tract contains some of the most magnificent glacial scenery in the Adirondack Park. It is characterized by a series of deep water ponds and lakes separated by a magnificently steep, conifer-clad esker—features with their origin in the last glacial age. Indeed, glacial topography reaches its apex here—truly the crown jewel of the northern region.

The tract was the site of the elegant Childwold Park Hotel. Recognizing the region's scenic splendor, turn of the century New York City society helped this hotel become one of the most fashionable resorts in upstate New York. Passengers on the New York Central Railroad came directly from Grand Central to the hamlet of Childwold, where they switched to the Grasse River Railroad to arrive at the hotel over a spur of this diminutive line that served primarily as a logging railroad.

Because of the remoteness of its location, the hotel was almost a complete self-contained entity. Fields and livestock supplied most of the meat and vegetables consumed by guests. The hotel's farm, called the Usher Farm, had originally been established by the Potsdam Lumber Company to serve its logging operations in the area. Only old apple trees tell of the farm's existence, and crumbling foundations offer mute witness to the grandeur that was once Childwold Park.

Except during the summer months (the last week in June through the last week in August), when the Scouts are in residence, the public can enjoy diverse recreational opportunities here. A permit is required for fishing and hunting; one can be obtained at the camp superintendent's office. The best adventure is a canoe trek on Massawepie Lake and down its outlet for a short way. Unplowed roads offer great cross-country skiing.

The entrance is on the west side of NY 3, approximately 6 miles east of Sevey Corners, or 5.3 miles west of the bridge over the Raquette River at Piercefield. The entrance area was once the site of a settlement called Gale, named after the first family to settle in the area in 1864.

85 Massawepie's Main Road and Its Ponds
Canoeing, fishing, cross-country skiing, map XVI

The private park's six-mile-long main road gives access to nine lakes that are intensively managed for trout. For several miles it follows the winding course of a serpentine esker. The region's crown jewels, strewn below the esker, have both prosaic names like Long, Round, Deer, or Pine, or more imaginative ones like Boot Tree, Horseshoe, Catamount, and Massawepie itself. (Massawepie is an Indian name for large water.) The ponds are frequently in sight from the roadway.

The ponds are linked together by informal carry trails established by the Boy Scouts and all provide excellent fishing for brook trout. All the ponds are easily accessible, though the outlier, Pine Pond, requires a carry of 2 miles from a parking area on the east side of the road at Horseshoe Pond. With the exception of some posted restricted areas near camp buildings, the ponds may be explored at any time other than the summer months. At 6 miles the main road reaches the Yorkshire Tract.

86 Massawepie Lake
Canoeing, map XVI

The largest and namesake lake in the tract offers an 8-mile round-trip canoe trip, enhanced by the pine and hemlock ridges that rim the lake. Eskers define the boundaries of bogs adjacent to the lake. Three state-listed endangered species breed here: osprey, loon, and lake whitefish.

Drive, walk, or ski the 1.2 miles from NY 3 along the main gravel road to a trail on the right. This short spur leads down to a sandy beach where you can launch your canoe.

On your paddle southwest down the length of the lake to the far western bay, be prepared to encounter occasional high winds. The outlet flows from the western bay. How far you can paddle down it depends on beaver dams and other encumbrances. The Massawepie Park tract extends for over a mile along the outlet, and you can carry around any impediments you meet in this stretch. After you leave the park, you have to turn back when you encounter the first carry. Before that you glimpse the Massawepie Mire—one of the most expansive wetlands in the entire park, with marshes, open peatland, alder swales, and spruce-tamarack swamps interwoven to create an ecosystem not only, of course, worthy of protection, but beautiful.

Chandler Pond Wild Forest

IN 1845, A series of violent storms swept across the north country from Lake Ontario, spawning tornados in their wake. One of these tornados cut a swath a half mile wide from the northern edge of Cranberry Lake northeast, across the Grass River, through Sevey Corners, and on into Franklin County. Settlers remembered the grassy swath that ultimately resulted—it made an easy roadway and cleared land for farming. Today it is recalled in a number of ponds and streams that bear the name Windfall and in three hotels named Windfall, one of which was in Sevey Corners.

Perhaps it is the stands of evergreens that sprang up uniformly after the Windfall that today characterize part of the Chandler Pond Wild Forest north of Sevey Corners. To reach the wild forest, drive 2.6 miles north of Sevey Corners and NY 3 on NY 56.

There is a small patch of Wild Forest surrounding Church Pond to the north. It is totally surrounded by private land and currently inaccessible. However, in the Diamond-Lassiter agreement, the state has obtained a right-of-way through the tract to the north of the Chandler Pond Wild Forest that will give access to Church Pond from Chandler Pond. As of this writing, the route has not been determined.

87 Chandler Pond Wild Forest Snowmobile Trail

Cross-country skiing, deer yard
4.8 miles round trip, relatively level, map XVII

A red-marked snowmobile trail provides an excellent base for cross-country skiing and also serves as an introduction to the boreal forests. The trail along a road starts on the left side of NY 56. During non-winter months, it is accessible to four-wheel-drive vehicles.

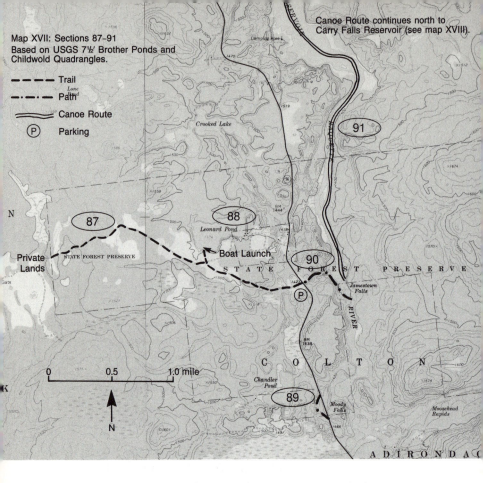

Map XVII: Sections 87–91
Based on USGS 7½' Brother Ponds and
Childwold Quadrangles.

- - - - Trail
- · - · - Path
======= Canoe Route
Ⓟ Parking

Canoe Route continues north to
Carry Falls Reservoir (see map XVIII).

Almost immediately, the trail enters a magnificent red pine plantation that reforested the area after the turn-of-the-century fires had denuded this tract. Notice how the understory shrub layer, particularly the red maple, has been pruned so repeatedly over the years that it has taken a bushy appearance. This area has one of the largest winter concentrations of deer in the park. The bushy growth of the shrubs in this deer yard result from intensive browsing of twigs and buds. The relative lack of snow and wind under these conifers entice the deer to areas like these where they have a better chance of surviving until spring. Still, the occasional hard Adirondack winter will kill dozens locally. Calling ravens locate the carcasses. Notice also the browse line on the understory balsam fir—the limit of the deer's winter reach.

At 0.7 mile, you ski through old fields in varying stages of recovery to forest. Nature has still not been able to reforest these fields opened by the fires. Scattered pin cherry, white pine, and black cherry are beginning the reforestation process, but large areas are covered only with bracken, blueberry, and reindeer lichen.

At 1 mile, a road comes in on the right—it leads back to private land on NY 56. The trail now passes a short spur to Leonard Pond at 1.2 miles and then continues on to dead-end at the boundary of state land at 2.7 miles. In the last stretch beyond the fields you pass an extensive spruce-fir swamp, dotted with tamarack, a good representative of a boreal woodland. Return to NY 56 on the same trail.

88 Leonard Pond

Canoeing, fishing, map XVII

Reached by a short 0.1-mile spur from the Chandler Pond Trail, 1.2 miles from NY 56, Leonard Pond is a splendid example of a glacial lake. Rimmed in part by cliffs covered with large hemlock and white pine, the pond lies wholly within the Forest Preserve, except for a small sliver of private land at the far end. A tiny, nearly circular island in the middle of the pond completes the boreal image.

89 Kettle Bog

Short path, map XVII

A tiny, classic Adirondack bog is easily explored from NY 56. At 1.4 miles from NY 3, a loop road goes to the right and returns in 0.2 mile to NY 56. The bog lies downslope from this loop road.

This classic kettle bog was formed when a disjointed chunk of ice lingered in the gravelly, sandy outwash for quite a while after the main covering of ice melted. When it finally did melt, it left the large depression that has been filling in ever since.

A three-layer concentric ring defines the bog. An outer layer of black spruce and tamarack surround a ring of open peatland—a matrix of sphagnum moss with layers of leatherleaf, Labrador tea, and insect-devouring pitcher plants. The open water in the middle is a dark pool, stained by tannin. Framing all this, towering white pine on the glacially deposited sandy slopes overlook the bog. All the elements of the more extensive peatland complexes of the boreal region are here gathered in miniature.

Raquette River and Carry Falls Reservoir

NIAGARA-MOHAWK POWER COMPANY built a hydroelectric dam across the Raquette River in the late 1940s and early 1950s to create the Carry Falls Reservoir. Trees were cut before the floodgates were closed; even the stumps were burned. The reservoir obliterated the old hamlet of Hollywood (named for the village in Ireland), where a charming inn was operated here by the Day family. It later became a dude ranch, which succumbed to the 1953 filling of the reservoir.

Carry Falls is but one of a series of dams on the Raquette built by Niagara-Mohawk. They stretch north to Higley and the village of Colton, which is just outside the park. NIMO maintains a chain of picnicking and camping sites along the river, all but one of which (Higley Pond) has a boat launch site. There is camping, for a fee, at two of them, the McNeil Campsite at Blake Pond Reservoir and the Parmenter Campsite at the head of Carry Falls Reservoir. The other fishing and picnic sites are located at Five Falls Pond, Rainbow Falls Pond, Stark Falls Pond, and Piercefield Flow, all points along the Raquette River and its impoundments.

State land touches Carry Falls Reservoir only at one point on its western shore. However, recent state purchases of Diamond International Company's holdings add a key link that stretches to the Jordan River. Further, the state has obtained recreation easements to land still held by Diamond to the east of Carry Falls. While the recreational potential of these lands has yet to be explored, it certainly will figure extensively in future editions of this guide.

Leonard Pond

Jamestown Falls

90 Raquette River–Jamestown Falls
Waterfalls, ski path, map XVII

Directly opposite the Chandler Pond Snowmobile Trail on NY 56 is a short, 0.3-mile spur road that leads to the Raquette River just below where an impressive, wide cascade tumbles into a long, wide pool. The road, which may be skied in winter, passes various glacial land forms on its descent to the river. Fishing for northern pike and smallmouth bass is good here, but it is best to fish from a boat. The shortness of the path makes it easy to carry a canoe to the river.

91 Raquette River–Carry Falls Reservoir
Canoeing, fishing, maps XVII and XVIII

An enjoyable, scenic 9-mile canoe trip can be made downstream from Jamestown Falls along the Raquette River. It ends at Carry Falls Reservoir on a tiny dot of state land just before the dam, where there is a public boat launching site.

Carry your canoe to the pool below Jamestown Falls. There is a long island immediately opposite the put-in. The first 1.5 miles are through Forest Preserve, with the river framed by majestic white pine and hemlock. This state land is part of the original Forest Preserve and the timber on them is truly impressive.

Be careful in this stretch, especially after Labor Day when the reservoir is lowered, for the river here was formerly the site of two formidable cataracts—Long Rapids and Halls Rapids (probably Hawes originally).

Beyond the Forest Preserve land, you pass the Parmenter Campsite operated by Niagara Mohawk throughout the summer. This spot, 2 miles along the river, is an alternate put-in; access is from a road forking from NY 56.

The river now begins to widen out into the reservoir, but the vistas are still handsome, particularly at high water during the summer. Several low mountains form the horizon. The appeal of the flow is enhanced by several small islands that dot the reservoir. Despite the regular drawdown of water, there is enough fish life for an odd pair of loons, bald eagles, and osprey.

You pass the mouth of the Jordan River after 5 miles. It is not navigable because of rapids in the first mile upstream. There is also no carry here because private lands surrounding the rapids are posted. Another mile along the Raquette brings you back to Forest Preserve land at Little Cold Brook. This is the start of the Bear Brook Trail—a 3-mile carry trail to the Jordan River put-in.

Another 3 miles of paddling across the reservoir takes you to the launch site. High winds and motorboats can be a hazard on this manmade lake. Either return to the Raquette River or take out here. It is 1 mile on Carry Falls Road to a left on Stark Road, and 1.5 miles along it to County Route 56. From here it is 15 miles south, left, to NY 3.

92 Bear Brook Trail

8.2 miles round trip, map XVIII

This isolated trail goes through and links several disjunct northern Forest Preserve parcels. It provides access to the Jordan River at the same time allowing you to explore some boreal terrain and enjoy a singular solitude that is all too rare.

The trail's isolation is explained by its beginning—it is reached only by a 6-mile canoe paddle on Carry Falls Reservoir after a put-in on the tote road

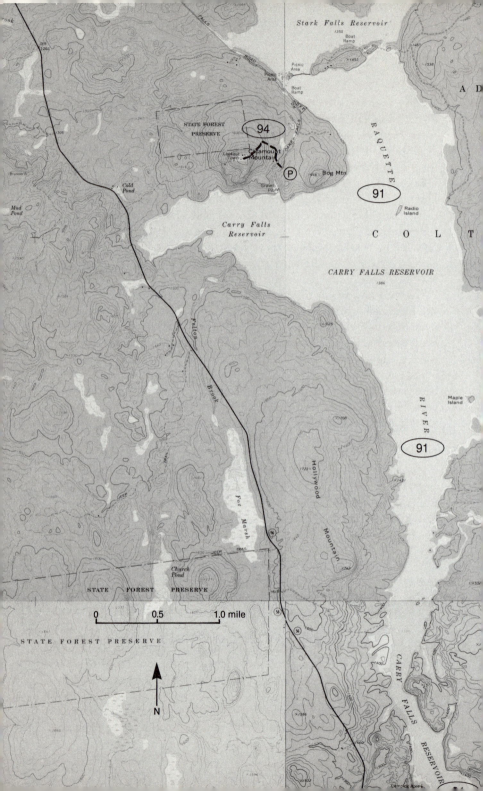

Stark Falls Reservoir

Boat Ramp

Picnic Area

Boat Ramp

STATE FOREST PRESERVE

94

Lookout Tower

Catamount Mountain

P

Gravel Pit

Bog Mtn

Cold Pond

Mud Pond

Carry Falls Reservoir

RAQUETTE

91

Radio Island

COLT

CARRY FALLS RESERVOIR

Fallon Brook

RIVER

Maple Island

91

Hollywood Mountain

Fox Marsh

JEEP

JEEP TRAIL

Church Pond

STATE FOREST PRESERVE

56

0   0.5   1.0 mile

STATE FOREST PRESERVE

N

56

56

CARRY FALLS RESERVOIR

AD

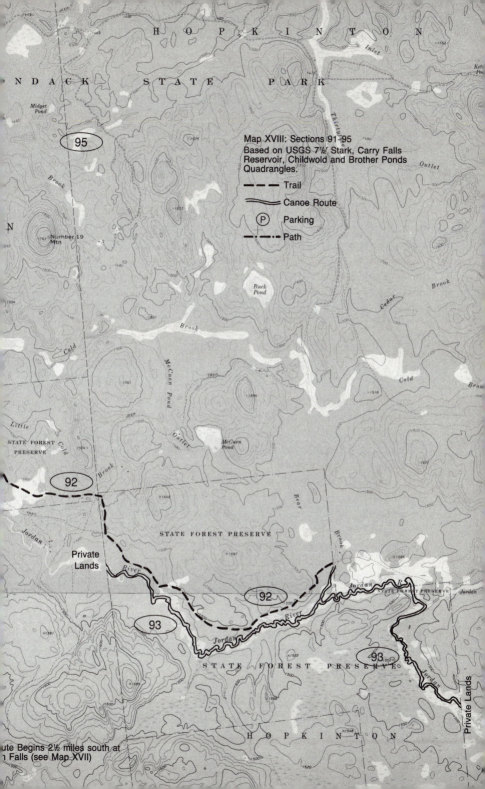

H O P K I N T O N

Inlet

N D A C K   S T A T E   P A R K

Outlet

Thirty

95

Midget
Pond

Brook

Brook

Map XVIII: Sections 91-95
Based on USGS 7½' Stark, Carry Falls
Reservoir, Childwold and Brother Ponds
Quadrangles.

Number 19
Mtn

Buck
Pond

Brook

Trail
Canoe Route
Ⓟ Parking
Path

Cold

Brook

McCuen Pond

Cold

Little Cold

STATE FOREST
PRESERVE

Outlet

McCuen
Pond

Brook

92

Brook

Bear

Jordan

Private
Lands

River

STATE FOREST PRESERVE

Brook

Jordan R.
STATE FOREST PRESERVE

Jordan

93

Jordan

92

River

93

Jordan

Jordan

Private Lands

S T A T E   F O R E S T   P R E S E R V E

H O P K I N T O N

ute Begins 2½ miles south at
n Falls (see Map XVII)

leading from NY 56 (section 91). During summer months, you can shorten the paddle to 4 miles by putting in at the Niagara-Mohawk Parmenter Campsite. The trail begins where Little Cold Brook flows into Carry Falls Reservoir, just at a point where state land touches the reservoir. The trail, long overgrown, has recently been reopened by the St. Lawrence County trail crew. A DEC sign marks the beginning.

The trail undulates through mixed northern forest for 3 miles, then crosses Whiskey Brook near where a side trail leads 50 yards to the Jordan River. If you can carry a canoe this far you can enjoy a great trip on that river (see section 93).

The trail continues on to cross Bear Brook in another mile. It ends at 4.1 miles, at the end of Forest Preserve land. The final 2 miles of trail are part of the old Hollywood-Tupper Lake road via Childwold.

93   Jordan River Canoe Trip
Map XVIII

A small, intimate, winding river that drains some of the finest boreal woodlands and wetlands in the park, the Jordan is surely a hidden treat. It is only a treat, however, for those willing and able to endure a 3-mile carry. From here a paddle of 6 to 8 miles can be made upriver and, depending on conditions, downriver as well.

The only encumbrances are usually an occasional fallen log or beaver dam. Progress is finally blocked by rapids and private land downriver and by narrowing, rapids, and private land upriver. Between, however, those who delight in the brooding majesty of spruce and fir will be satiated. But the beginning, 6 miles by canoe over Carry Falls Reservoir and 3 miles along an occasionally muddy Bear Brook Trail, means that few will ever enjoy it.

94   Catamount Mountain
Trail, easy climb
1.3 miles, map XVIII

Catamount is the highest summit in the Raquette River region between Moosehead Mountain and Potsdam to the north. It is Colvin's "Bog

Mountain," first occupied by the Adirondack Survey in 1879 and again in 1883. (The 7.5-minute Carry Falls USGS map shows a lower Bog Mountain east of Catamount, thus closer to the large bog flooded by the Carry Falls Reservoir; however, the visibility of Colvin's Bog Mountain from Mt. Azure and Mt. Morris to the east, and from Baldface Mountain to the west, justifies its selection as a "central point of reference" in Colvin's triangulation network, and establishes it as today's Catamount. The placing of two successive fire towers and several survey bolts on Catamount support this conclusion. Naming the lower Bog Mountain closer to the bog is evidently local usage.)

A noted hotel, the Mountain House, was located at the foot of the mountain in the late nineteenth century. The hotel, operated by the Fenton family, entertained famous guests, including Julia Crane, the founder of the Crane School of Music, located at Potsdam, New York.

A short, easy trail to the top of this low mountain rewards the climber with a panoramic view of Stark Reservoir and of the vast, mostly boreal woodlands stretching east of the reservoir well into Franklin County. Although there is a parcel of state land on the far flanks of the mountain, the top and the trail to it are all on private land. Care and good stewardship on the trail will ensure that access remains open to the public.

Access is from Stark Road, 1.5 miles east of its intersection with County Route 56. This intersection is approximately 15 miles north of NY 3. Take a right onto Hollywood (Carry Falls) Road and continue 1 mile to a turnaround and boat launching site for Carry Falls Reservoir. Walk straight ahead from here on a dirt road, which is a remnant of the Old Hollywood Road that formerly went to Childwold station on the New York Central.

After 0.8 mile, the dirt road ends with a house straight ahead. The 0.5-mile trail to the top starts to the right of the house. There is a sharp left turn just before the summit, where you can see the foundations of an old fire tower and cabin, structures that were removed fifteen years ago. Their removal does not limit your view of the countryside.

95 Kildare Tract
Map XVIII

Lying east of Carry Falls Reservoir, this tract is part of the recent Diamond-Lassiter acquisition. It consists of 3500 acres purchased by the state and 15,800 acres on which the state holds an easement. Exclusive hunting rights are to be retained by the existing sportsmen's clubs for a thirty-year period, but all other recreation rights are available to the public, including fishing.

At present, the only access to this tract is a bushwhack of about a mile through mostly old growth white pine and hemlock stands in the Jordan River Wild Forest, after a canoe trip across the Raquette River. The Lassiter Corporation has two years in which to provide suitable public access to the parcel and if they do not the state will step in and provide it. At this time, it appears that access will probably be provided from the Joe Indian Pond Road, a town road lying mostly north of the tract.

Stone Dam Wild Forest

THIS ISOLATED PARCEL of Forest Preserve attracts hunters and snow-mobilers and has limited appeal to hikers who wish to explore such a remote place. The only access to this 2600-acre, land-locked parcel is currently over an old town road with a public right-of-way. DEC has marked the route as a snowmobile trail and it receives heavy use from all-terrain vehicles during the hunting season.

To find the trail, take County Route 115 for 2.3 miles from the hamlet of DeGrasse to a right fork, just past a metal bridge, onto Dean Road. Go 5.8 miles on Dean Road, noting where the old road comes in on the left, just past the building complex of a hunting club.

96 Stone Dam Wild Forest Access Road

Cross-country skiing, river exploration, snowmobile trail, map XIX

The road/trail proceeds in a rolling fashion for 2.6 miles beyond the hunting club to the state land boundary. In another 0.2 mile, it reaches the Middle Branch of the Grass River. The main portion of the tract lies across the river, which can be forded, carefully, in low water. There is an unofficial crude wooden bridge placed across by hunters and sometimes a cable crossing, but neither are certain ways to cross. A cable is often placed at the site of the Old Stone Dam, which was constructed to create an impoundment known as a "jack-works," which held back cut logs prior to their being sent downriver to the mills in early spring.

The river flows for 1.5 miles through state lands and you can enjoy an amble along it. This is quite special, because sportsmen's clubs lease from corporate owners and post the rest of the land on all three branches of the Grass, which is among the most wild and scenic in the park.

Map XIX: Section 96
Based on USGS 7½' Tooley Pond and
Albert Marsh Quadrangles.

– – – Trail
——— Road

Cross-country Skiing and Snowmobile Trail

96

Dean Rd
←5mi.
to Rt. 115
Gooseberry
Mtn

STATE FOREST PRESERVE

STATE FOREST
PRESERVE

MIDDLE BRANCH GRASS RIVER

Tunkethandle
Hill

Blue Mountain

C O L

Pleasant Lake

Mile
Pond

Tracy
Brook

Falls

Rapids

Rapids

Tracy
Pond

Deerskin
Pond

Deerskin Cr

Mud Brook

Goblet
Spring

Lower Camp

Brook

C L A R E

0   0.5   1.0 mile

N

Clear Pond Wild Forest

THIS REMOTE AND fairly large parcel of Forest Preserve land lies outside what is usually considered the low elevation boreal biome, but it is characterized by the same coniferous forests and peatlands that they possess. The boreal vegetation here stems from the generally unproductive sandy soils and the microclimate of many frost pockets with extremes that can rival those of the High Peaks region on occasion.

An abandoned settlement called Picketville lies buried deep in the tract. Named after a mid-nineteenth-century settler, houses and a schoolhouse stood along Picketville Road. The road was abandoned after 1920 and all that remains today are old foundations and gnarled apple trees. The road once crossed the Raquette River on a bridge at a particularly scenic spot. That, too, is now gone and the river has become the Rainbow Falls Reservoir.

Clear Pond Wild Forest is reached via Stark Road (which becomes Joe Indian Road). Go 12.1 miles from the intersection of Stark Road and County Route 56 to a dirt road on the left marked by two pillars. You can still drive 1.9 miles down the dirt road through Forest Preserve land to the abandoned buildings of the Camp Vigor Boy Scout complex. Hiking trails begin on the right of the camp.

In winter you can ski the road to the camp—there is usually a snowmobile base. It leads past a beaver pond, then up a winding esker lined with huge white pine, and past a haunting spruce-tamarack swamp on the right. Beyond the esker on the left lies a large, open peatland—its snowy stillness etched white on white, in contrast to the bog in summer when the only white visible are waving plumes of cotton grass.

97 Clear Pond
Swimming, fishing, camping, map XX

This medium-sized, circular pond, also known as Vigor Pond, has recently been the scene of an interesting experiment in wildlife management. When the state acquired the tract a few years ago, it was determined that the pond had the physical and chemical properties needed to support a

native brook trout fishery. The trout, however, could not compete with the abundant and stunted non-native species that had proliferated. In the summer of 1988, rotenone was used to kill all forms of fish life. Brook trout will be stocked and their progress will be closely followed.

The camp outbuildings are considerably dilapidated and will be removed now that the state has acquired the tract. Meanwhile, the sandy beach can be enjoyed by all and the public can camp nearby.

98 Big Rock Pond

Snowmobile trail, hiking, cross-country skiing
5.8 miles round trip, map XX

This trail is the main one through the Clear Pond Wild Forest. It begins at the end of the gravel road on the shores of Clear Pond and proceeds along the shore following red DEC disks. At 0.3 mile it forks right (left goes to Little Rock Pond, section 99).

The trail is generally clear and fairly wide—quite suitable for cross-country skiing. A second-growth mixed forest covers most of the trail. After approximately 2 miles, you cross the outlet of Big Rock Pond on a beaver dam. Due to the deteriorating condition of the dam, Big Rock Pond is today mostly a cattail-sedge marsh, an open vly with water only at the upper end.

The trail continues another 0.9 mile to end at a junction with Picketville Road, near where the old schoolhouse once stood.

If the skiing is good and the weather pleasant, particularly if a snowmobile base is present on Picketville Road, you may wish to make a left turn here and go an additional 2.8 miles down Picketville Road to Rainbow Falls Reservoir. The way is mostly through Forest Preserve with an occasional hunting camp. Return on the same routes, making an 11.4-mile round trip to the reservoir, so be sure you have enough daylight.

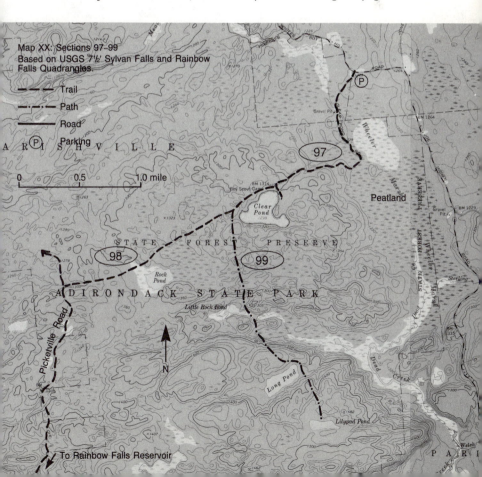

99   Little Rock, Long, and Lilypad Ponds

Trail, hiking, fishing
2.6 miles round trip to Little Rock Pond; 4.8 miles additional
round trip to Lilypad Pond on a newly flagged route, map XX

A trail to Little Rock Pond branches from the Big Rock Pond Trail, 0.3 mile from its beginning and just past the shores of Clear Pond. It follows red paint and sporadic DEC snowmobile discs. Various disks and mileage posts survive from Boy Scout days, but they are not particularly accurate.

The path goes up and over several ridges through a mostly beech-cherry forest. After 1.3 miles and a sharp descent you reach the outlet of Little Rock Pond, which lies in the valley between two ridges. It is eutrophied to the point that it is a conifer-ringed marsh with relatively little open water—the result of a natural process that ultimately will befall all such shallow ponds.

Recently, the old, overgrown trail linking the network of interior ponds in the Clear Pond Wild Forest has been rehabilitated and rerouted by DEC. The trails connecting these tiny jewels in the forest were maintained by the Boy Scout Camp, which owned the tract. A new route has been marked by DEC and there are plans to clear and brush out a trail along the marked route in late 1989. At present, the markers end at Lilypad Pond. Ultimately, the trail will be extended another 3.5 miles along a currently overgrown, wet, hunters' path to Rainbow Falls Reservoir and then possibly back to Clear Pond via Picketville Road for a total loop of 15 miles.

For now, you can follow the flagged route. Head downslope from the boulder at the outlet of Little Rock Pond along the overgrown path for about 100 yards to a line of blue markers. Occasional red discs supplement the blue ribbons. The path begins a gradual ascent up one of the highest ridges in the area. Some of the sugar maples right beside the path are approaching the maximum girth of this official New York State tree. On the top of the ridge, poplars are succumbing to old age and beech are dying from fungus.

The markers descend to reach Long Pond, 1.7 miles from Little Rock Pond. Despite its small size—seven acres—Long Pond is the largest of the interior ponds. A half dozen species of dragonflies glide and swoop over the open water, while deerflies and mosquitos appear frenzied as they relentlessly harass a summer hiker.

Little Rock Pond

From Long Pond, the route goes over another ridge, this one crowned with large beech, before descending to Lilypad Pond in another 0.7 mile. This three-acre gem is bordered with balsam fir and hemlock. Despite their small size, both ponds are stocked with brook trout and fishing is reputed to be excellent.

Return, for now, to Little Rock Pond, though in the future you may be able to go to Rainbow Falls.

Tooley Pond Road

BUILT IN 1864, Tooley Pond Road was the first road to lead from the Adirondack lowlands to Cranberry lake. Today it is a winding, bumpy, partly macadam road connecting the hamlets of Cranberry lake and DeGrasse. It generally parallels the South Branch of the Grass River. For almost all its length it passes through woodlands leased to sportsmen's clubs and is off-limits to the public. It does, however, provide interesting views and frequent sightings of wildlife, canoe launch sites, and a pleasant drive.

100 Tooley Pond Road
Drive with river view, wildlife, and canoe put-in
18 miles

Starting from Cranberry Lake, the road comes to a wide, sandy boat ramp in 0.5 mile. Here on the left, canoes may be launched for a 5-mile paddle along the Main Branch of the Oswegatchie River, with a take-out after several short carries at the beach in Newton Falls, where an industrial dam has widened the river and created extensive wetlands along its basin. The voyage is reminiscent of lake paddling in many respects, but with numerous sightings of wildlife, loons, blue herons, ring-necked ducks, and green wing teal.

At 2.6 miles you pass through a crossroads hunting hamlet called Cooks Corner. This was also on the path of the most disastrous tornado ever to strike the area. The 1845 tornado leveled the half-mile-wide swath that beckoned homesteaders to try subsistence farming in the cleared swath. After less than a generation, inclement weather and poor soils prevailed. The only visible signs of this are some foundations and a 7-mile long thoroughfare known as the Windfall Road. This road, used by hunting clubs and loggers, goes from Cooks Corner to NY 3 at the Grass River Bridge and is entirely off-limits to the public. There is still a Windfall Restaurant in Cooks Corners.

Tooley Road proceeds to Tooley Pond, a beautiful glacial sheet of water at 5.8 miles. Tooley Pond Mountain, seen looming above the lake, once had a fire tower and a public trail. Both are no more. The pond, road, and mountain were named for an early woodsman, as were so many of the area's features.

All along the road you see signs of lumbering—hardwood trees replacing the original conifers (except in the wetlands). Log and skid roads lead into the forest of mostly small trees. White-tailed deer prefer the herbs of the open areas where harvesting has been intensive, and they are sustained in winter by feeding programs of some of the hunting clubs.

At 9.1 miles, the road bridges the Grass River. The road follows the river, but you rarely see it, except between 13.2 and 13.7 miles. At 14 miles, you pass a split waterfall, but it is so posted you cannot even go close enough to get a good look at it. Some of the most magnificent waterfalls in the park lie along the Grass River here—both above and below Tooley Pond Road. All the public can now enjoy of them are brief glimpses, such as the one at 15 miles, where a dirt road to the left provides a thrilling view of a falls as it cascades over a precipice under the bridge.

At 17 miles, Tooley Pond Road ends on County Route 115. Turn left and drive 0.3 mile to reach DeGrasse.

Grass River Wild Forest

JUST BEFORE THE Grass River, or the union of its South and Middle branches, leaves the Adirondack Park for the second time, it enters a patch of land acquired by the state in 1979. Here the river flows over one of the northern Adirondacks' most impressive waterfalls. As if that were not enough, the river tumbles through a series of cataracts, flumes, ravines, and falls that is unequaled in the park. And to top it off, an exceptionally fine trail winds along beside the river, giving access to the entire series of visual delights.

The river here is entrenched in a fold with periodic gneisses and marbles, and the falls themselves are interlayered gneiss and marble. A series of smoothly worn rock shelves creates the falls and the downstream cascades.

Old maps show the river spelled with a final e, but somehow it has been lost, even though the hamlet of DeGrasse retains it.

101 Lampson Falls

Short trail, picnic spot
0.5 mile, 10 minutes, level walking, map XXI

Head north from Degrasse on County Route 77, cross the Grass River, and pass Tooley Pond Road at 0.5 mile. At 4.6 miles, a sign on the west side of the road marks an entrance to the Grass River Wild Forest. Blue markers denote the trail that follows an old road west, past a cedar swamp on the right, posted lands on the left. A few big pines and hemlock line the roadway and crown a rocky knoll to the right. The road curves and in seven minutes you begin to hear Lampson Falls. The road branches left to the flow above the falls and right to split into paths leading beside the falls and to the pool below it. Anyway you go you will be charmed by the view.

Lampson Falls is a broad sheet of water falling over a smooth, rounded rock formation that is some thirty feet tall. Huge cedars lean over the deep

pool below the falls. The continuing red trail crosses a tiny stream on a bridge and climbs another knoll with the aid of a staircase that leads to campsites on its crest. The trail drops again to water level and a picnic spot on a rocky peninsula below.

102 Grass River Trails

2.6 miles of trail offering 4.4 miles hiking, 3 or more hours, relatively level, yellow canoe-carry and red markers, map XXI

Leave Lampson Falls heading north through a marshy hemlock grove. You cross a wet area with a bog off to your right then pass some huge maples and an alder meadow with great stands of osmunda ferns. Several little log bridges and chains of planks help you cross wet areas and a little stream. Up to your right you can see a rocky bluff that echoes the formation under the falls.

The trail continues close to shore. Flatwater ends and as you begin to hear rapids again you see a rock island and a bridge ahead. Watch out for poison ivy as you approach the bridge 0.8 mile from Lamspon Falls, about twenty minutes. A roadway comes in from the right; a path leads ahead and you can use it to explore the river downstream; but for the best walk along the river, cross the bridge. A left turn across the bridge is a red trail that leads you back upstream almost a mile to the east shore of Lampson Falls. Here you will find a picnic site on the pine-covered bluffs that is more secluded than the more accessible area close to the road.

Below the bridge, the river is squeezed between two smooth rock ledges. Turning right, and following yellow canoe-carry markers now, you climb a narrow path along a ridge, then descend to a sandy bay at the end of a small stillwater. This ends in a narrow flume, followed by a second, deeper flume. A log bench provides a place to rest and look at this falls. Another stretch of quiet water is broken when a rock island splits the river, forcing half into a deep flume, the west half over a rocky cascade. The rhythm of rock outcrops quickening the river and the quiet of deep flows below each cascade continues. There is one deep canyon stretch below which the river broadens with a steep rock slide on the opposite shore. Pools, eddies, and oxbows overhung with cedars follow. Sandy beaches quickly disappear in the dark, tannin-stained water. Another rock island splits the river, which is very turbulent below.

Below another waterfall, the river broadens into wider rapids and begins to curve. The trail enters a reforestation area and hangs left, while a path stays right and is more obvious. Another broad and jumbled waterfall follows, and immediately the river splits, with the near flow plunging into a narrow canyon. Deep in a maple woods, the river suddenly becomes more placid as it completes the hairpin curve and heads southwest, leaving state land 0.8 mile from the bridge.

When you return upstream, you can vary the trip by staying on the west bank and continuing to the head of Lampson Falls—watch out for the holes of bank beaver in the trail if you do. Or, you can cross the bridge and follow the path downstream until it peters out, watching the changing moods of the river from a different perpsective.

103 Harpers Falls

Short walk, path, waterfall
0.6 mile, fifteen minutes, mild grade, map XXI

The North Branch of the Grass River also plunges from the Adirondack highlands near the park boundary. A patch of state land surrounds Harpers

Falls, the punctuation point in that plunge. Continue north of DeGrasse, past the trail to Lampson Falls for 2.8 miles to Donnerville Road, and turn left. The dirt road through the gravel pit has been washed out in the past and the road to the right out of it is not in the best shape, so it may be better to park here and walk the 0.55 mile to the left turn along an old road, which will take you to the falls. If you drive, there is limited parking at the turnoff, which is clearly marked as state land.

The old road is gated; follow it as it heads gradually downhill, across a small stream, then up a knoll and down again into a valley. It only takes ten minutes or so to reach the river. To the right is a messy area where people have camped too close to water. Downstream the river widens out. Upstream, however, there are actually two falls and some fascinating rock work to explore. You can clearly find the channel for a sluiceway that diverted water to a long-gone mill, whose foundations are built of beautifully cut rocks.

If you follow Donnerville Road west across the blue line and outside the park, you pass the site of the abandoned village of Donneville. Another logging road leads to the North Branch and recent acquisitions have made this stretch of river from Harpers Falls almost to the confluence with the Main Branch open to the public, something that is especially welcomed by fishermen.

Harpers Falls on the North Branch Grass River

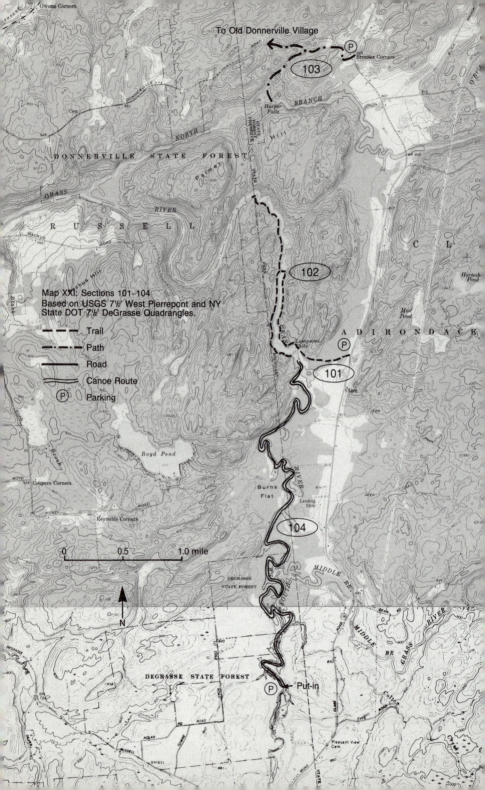

Northern State Forests

LYING JUST OUTSIDE the boundaries of the Adirondack Park are a number of State Forests or State Reforestation areas that are managed under an entirely different principle than the Forest Preserve lands of the park. These forests, which offer a variety of recreational opportunities, are managed on a multiple use theory that stresses equally timber harvesting and public recreation. The timber is marked by a state forester and logged under contract by private companies. The logging assures a higher population of certain wildlife, especially deer, but you will also find hare and grouse and even black bear. The true wilderness species—marten, lynx, moose, and bobcat—fare much better under the protective shield of the Forest Preserve, where forests are never cut.

Among the hidden joys of the northwestern Adirondacks are the long flows of various rivers and creeks that drain the extended plateau that gradually slopes to the lowlands of the St. Lawrence Valley. Several of these rivers flow through the State Forests and are great for canoeing or river ambles. The State Forests in this chapter each have such delightful rivers.

104 DeGrasse State Forest
Grass River Canoe Route, waterfall
9 miles round trip, map XXI

The three branches of the Grass River are distinguished by long flows through corporately owned forests that are leased exclusively to hunting clubs. Only a sampler of this magnificent river can be enjoyed at a point where the river begins to prepare for its rapid descent from the Adirondack Plateau. The trip begins in the DeGrasse River State Forest and ends just before Lampson Falls in the Grass River Wild Forest (section 101), after the river has meandered back into the Adirondack Park for its exciting plunge to cross the park boundary again.

The canoe trip begins at a launching area in the DeGrasse State Forest. Take County Route 38 for 1.1 miles past its intersection with County Routes 77 and 115 in the hamlet of DeGrasse and make a right turn, taking it to the end at a parking area in a pine plantation. Small signs point the way to the canoe launching site straight ahead.

Head downriver through a handsome white spruce plantation on the left. There are a few private inholdings along the river, but they are quickly forgotten as the river winds its way through scenic forests. Especially handsome is the long esker bordering the right bank with its crown of towering hemlock. The sandy, eroded sides of the esker are home to a colony of bank swallows, which will noisily dart around your canoe in early summer. You may see beaver swimming in the river, but their dams do not impede the flow here. The river is too wide and swift to be tamed by beaver. Rather, they make their dens in the sand banks along the shores.

About halfway to Lampson Falls, the Middle Branch of the Grass comes

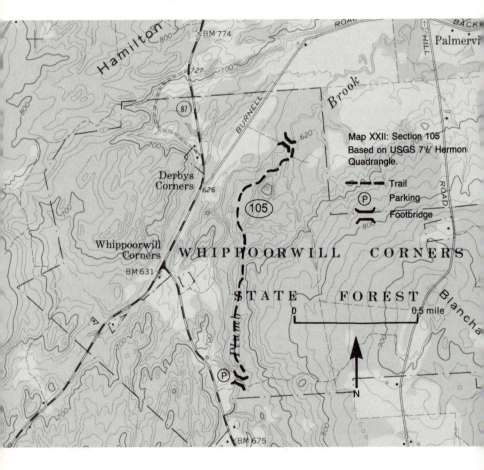

in on the right. A wide floodplain lined with silver maples and occasional cottonwood defines the meeting of the waters here. You can canoe upriver on the Middle Branch for a short distance, until fallen logs block further progress.

At 4.5 miles, listen carefully for the falls ahead, and take out on the right just before the foundation of an old power house building—there are no signs here, so be careful—the falls are straight ahead! From here it is an easy 0.3-mile carry out to County Route 115 (see section 101), or you can return upriver to the State Forest. In either event there is a splendid picnic spot on the left bank under towering white pines overlooking the falls. Breathe deeply and enjoy, for in other areas commercial establishments have been built solely to capitalize on views decidedly inferior to this.

105 Whippoorwill Corners State Forest
Plumb Brook Trail, fishing
2.8 miles round trip, red markers, map XXII

If you go another 4.2 miles on County Route 38 past the entrance to the DeGrasse State Forest (section 104) you reach the entrance to the Whippoorwill Corners State Forest on the right. The entrance is 5.3 miles from DeGrasse; straight ahead is the crossroads of Whippoorwill Corners.

Both the State Forest and the crossroads were named for the nocturnal bird with its haunting call. These birds were once abundant here.

Proceed down a dirt road from the entrance to a small parking lot near the banks of Plumb Brook. The river amble begins here after the trail crosses over the brook on a footbridge.

The brook is forty to fifty feet wide, almost a river. It is stocked with brown and brook trout; there is excellent fishing from its bank. There are small waterfalls near the beginning of the walk downstream, then the river alternates between rapids and flat water for the remainder of its route through the state forest.

Occasional yellow fishing markers are interspersed with the red ones along the trail. The DEC sign says it is 1.2 miles between bridges, but the way is actually longer. Hemlock-clad cliffs come down to the brook in several areas and large white pine are also present, but not the giants of the forests around Wanakena. Basswood and wild grape remind you that you are not in a typical Adirondack forest, but in a lowland one where the land was once farmed. The trail ends at a second footbridge spanning Plumb Brook. Such a streamside ramble as this is all too rare in the region.

Greenwood Falls

106 Greenwood Creek State Forest

Waterfall, picnic area
2.1-mile loop trail, map XXIII

Greenwood State Forest is 1.3 miles from NY 3 along Greenwood Falls Road, which is 8.4 miles east of the village of Harrisville or 15 miles west of the village of Star Lake. This medium-sized reforestation area lies astride the western boundary of the Adirondack Park. The forest is highlighted by an exceptionally pleasant picnic area nestled under a canopy of red pines and facing a twenty-foot cataract that plunges over bedrock into a placid pool, right beside the picnic area. The pines were planted in hayfields here during the Depression years by the Civilian Conservation Corps. Much of the bedrock in this peripheral Adirondack area has a high component of calcareous marble, hence the soils are less acidic than most Adirondack soils. The flora has a greater diversity than most mountain places. In spring you will see hepaticas, wild ginger, and white trillium.

A short nature trail begins at the picnic area. A spur with yellow disks goes south for 0.3 mile to a wooden observation platform that overlooks

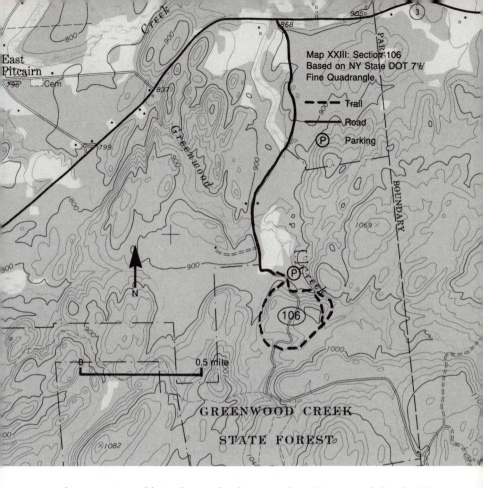

the expansive alder-sedge wetland surrounding Greenwood Creek. Blue heron are frequently sighted here and you may hear the weird water-pump call of the American Bittern even if he remains camouflaged in the sedges. Perhaps you can take a brook trout here for supper. Return to the falls for the main nature trail loop.

The 2.1-mile nature trail starts south from the picnic area and ascends a rock ridge along the shores of Greenwood Creek. The fissures in the cliffs across the creek are visited by bobcat in winter and early spring. After leaving the red pine plantation, the trail turns from the creek and heads up a hardwood ridge. In late spring, before the leaves come out, the forest floor is covered with hepatica, dutchman's breeches, and white trillium, all flowers that thrive on the relatively non-acidic soils.

You pass a dug-out spring. It was first constructed by the CCC in the 1930s and rebuilt by the St. Lawrence Youth Conservation Corp in the early 1980s. Summer algae covering the open water may make it unfit for drinking, however.

Put-in

Put-in

Map XXIV: Section 107.
Based on USGS 7½ Remington Corners
Quadrangle.

- - - - Trail

〜〜〜 Canoe Route

──── Road

Ⓟ Parking

Kimballs Mills Road

107-1A

JADWIN MEMORIAL STATE FOREST

Tinney Corners

107-2A

107-3

To Lassiter

107-1A

Blanchard

Also shown on Map VIII

107-2B

C R O G H A N

N

0   0.5   1.0 mile

Put-in

Jerden Falls

107-1B

JADWIN MEMORIAL STATE FOREST

Canoe Route continues 5 miles south.

Signs explain various silvicultural practices, among them thinning and cutting for pulp wood.

The trail crosses the main road at 1 mile and continues along the slope on the opposite side. This slope has been left in a natural condition with large red oaks. After traversing some rock outcrops, the trail reaches a plantation of balsam fir and white spruce. The fir is a common native pioneering species, not often used for reforestation. The trail now follows a brook back across the road to the start of the loop at the picnic area.

107 Jadwin State Forest
Canoeing and cross-country skiing, map XXIV

Lying astride the western Park boundary is the sprawling 20,000-acre Jadwin State Forest, named for Frank Jadwin, a former DEC forester. This reforestation area, characterized by pine plantations, spruce swamps, and beaver ponds, is managed by DEC under the multiple-use theory of lumbering and recreation. As a result, the forest has an extensive gravel road system, making even its distant corners very accessible. It has recently assumed added importance as a key public access to part of the recently acquired Diamond-Lassiter lands.

The forest has quite an interesting history. Many of its tracts were abandoned farmlands purchased by the state for $4 an acre during the Depression. A CCC camp located on present day NY 812 was established in the forest in 1934. It closed, then reopened in 1944 to house German prisoners of war, who were put to work harvesting pulp in the nearby forests.

Several abandoned settlements were located in what is now the State Forest. Among them were Kimball's Mill, Tinnly's Corners, and the inelegantly named hamlet of Pigtown. The latter was at one time the location of both a tannery and a sawmill. These tiny settlements usually had their own schools and cemeteries and one of the schoolhouses remains as a hunting camp on the Kimball Mills Road just west of its junction with the Jerden Falls Road.

In addition to providing access to the Diamond-Lassiter lands, the Jadwin State Forest also offers a variety of recreational opportunities. The West Branch of the Oswegatchie River flows for miles through the forest and access is provided at several points by the gravel town roads that serve the forest. There are no marked hiking trails in the forest, but two DEC truck trails, generally now plowed in winter, make good cross-country ski loops, especially when they have a packed snowmobile base.

1—CANOEING THE WEST BRANCH OF THE OSWEGATCHIE

Rough parking areas have been constructed by DEC at two locations to provide access to the river for fishermen and canoeists.

A—*Kimballs Mills Road.* There are two access points to the river located along this road. Take NY 3 for 3 miles west of the village of Harrisville and turn south on NY 812 for 2.1 miles to a left turn onto Kimballs Mills Road. Follow that road for 1.5 miles to a small, unimproved parking area on the right. This is adjacent to the first launch site. The second is located 0.8 mile farther along on Kimballs Mills Road, also on the right.

Both of these areas offer short samplers of up to 0.5 mile of flat-water canoeing without carries, in both directions from either site. In spite of the nearby road, all is serene with both banks of the river lined with the red maple, spruce, and hemlock of the state forest. You will frequently see beaver. Wood ducks in their splendid plumage are visitors to the river. In June and early July, numerous warblers are identified by their songs even if their fluttering flight makes visible identification almost impossible. These short, but delightful stretches are a great introduction to a relatively unknown river.

B—*Jerden Falls Road.* With a little effort and luck, this can be a much longer foray on the West Branch. Go 2.4 miles beyond the second canoe put in on Kimballs Mills Road to Jerden Falls Road. Turn right at the T intersection and proceed for 3.5 miles to a metal bridge spanning the river. You can put in by carefully walking down the bank here. Although you can canoe a short way upriver here, the main route is downriver. At times of high water, depending on your perseverance and such impediments as beaver dams and stands of alders that narrow the channel, you can canoe downriver for about 6 miles or more, returning for a 12-mile round trip. There are a few, relatively short rapids.

2—CROSS-COUNTRY SKI TRAILS

A—*Main Truck Trail Loop.* This 4-mile-long loop leaves the Jerden Falls Road on the left, 0.1 mile from its intersection with the Kimballs Mills Road. It returns to the Jerden Falls Road 0.9 mile to the south. The truck trail ascends several small hills, but the width of the trail makes them suitable for novice skiers. Like most state forest truck trails, this one was constructed during the Depression with the two-fold objective of fire suppression and timber transportation.

The forest traversed by this loop is mainly red and white pine plantations with some Norway spruce. The road crosses Brown's Creek and passes extensive beaver marshes. At 2.1 miles, the loop swings right, while a side spur forks left for 0.2 mile to the barred gate denoting the beginning of the Diamond-Lassiter lands on which the state now holds a conservation easement.

B—Blanchard Creek Truck Trail. This 2.8-mile truck trail loop begins 0.6 mile farther south on Jerden Falls Road from the concluding leg of the Main Truck Trail Loop, or 1.6 miles from the intersection with Kimballs Mills Road. It circles back to Jerden Falls Road at a point 1.5 miles to the south.

The loop starts just past where Blanchard Creek tumbles in a pretty cascade under a small stone bridge on the Jerden Falls Road. The stone bridge was constructed during the CCC era, but the area's history dates to the latter half of the nineteenth century when a sawmill owned by a man named Blanchard was located here. Local lore tells that Blanchard founded this venture on riches he obtained in the California gold rush.

This truck trail loop has more hardwoods along its course than the main loop. Active logging plus stands of sugar maple and black cherry have led to a diverse wildlife population. You often spot the tracks of such predators as bobcats as well as the tracks of that large weasel, the fisher.

The return leads to the Jerden Falls Road a short distance north of the metal bridge over the Oswegatchie. As this road is erratically plowed in winter, you can walk back along it to your car, ski along its sides, or rerun the loop.

3—WESTERN ENTRANCE TO THE MIDDLE BRANCH OSWEGATCHIE TRACT

Bryant's Bridge Road forks right, east, from Jerden Falls Road just north of the bridge over the Middle Branch Oswegatchie. You can also reach Bryant's Bridge Road from Harrisville via Middle Branch Road. The road leads through lands still retained by the Lassiter Corporation; but they have granted an easement along this road to the Middle Branch Tract for canoers and kayakers only. The Middle Branch is a whitewater river here. However, there is a lovely waterfall, Rainbow Falls, near the western edge of the easement lands. When the extension of Bryant's Bridge Road is connected to the Bald Mountain Road, giving access from the south, hikers also will be able to enjoy these falls as well as this lovely stretch of the river and the numerous ponds in the northeastern portion of the Middle Branch Oswegatchie Tract. Bryant's Bridge Road winds east through the tract, crosses the Middle Branch on a bridge at Mullers Flow at the canoe put-in, and continues north toward the Aldrich Pond Wild Forest.

References and Other Resources

Allen, Richard S., William Gove, Keith F. Maloney, Richard F. Palmer. *Rails in the North Woods.* Sylvan Beach, New York: North Country Books, 1978.

Beetle, David H. *Up Old Forge Way.* Lakemont, New York: North Country Books, 1972. Reprinted 1984.

Clark, F. Mark. "The Low Dynasty." *The Quarterly* XIX (1), St. Lawrence County Historical Society, January 1974.

DeSormo, Maitland C. *Heydays of the Adirondacks.* Saranac Lake, New York: Adirondack Yesteryears, Inc., 1974.

Donaldson, Alfred L. *A History of the Adirondacks,* Volumes I and II. New York: Century Co., 1921; reprint, Harrison, New York: Harbor Hill Books, 1977.

Fowler, Albert. *Cranberry Lake, from Wilderness to Adirondack Park.* Syracuse, New York: The Adirondack Museum/Syracuse University Press, 1968.

Hammond, Samuel H. *Wild Northern Scenes, or Sporting Adventures in the Adirondacks with Rifle and Rod.* New York: Derby and Jackson, 1857; reprint, Harrison, New York: Harbor Hill Books, 1976.

Harter, Henry A. *Fairy Tale Railroad.* Sylvan Beach, New York: North Country Books, 1979.

Headley, Joel T. *The Adirondack; or, Life in the Woods.* Harrison, New York: Harbor Hill Books, 1982; facsimile of 1849 edition with introduction by Philip G. Terrie.

Jamieson, Paul. *Adirondack Canoe Waters.* Glens Falls, New York: The Adirondack Mountain Club, Inc., 1975.

Katz, E. C. "A Star in the Wilderness." *The Four-Track News,* June 1906.

Keith, Herbert F. *Man of the Woods.* With introduction by Paul Jamieson. Syracuse, New York: The Adirondack Museum/Syracuse University Press, 1972.

Kirschenbaum, Schafstall, and Stuchin, editors. *The Adirondack Guide.* Raquette Lake, New York: Sagamore Institute, 1983.

Kudish, Michael. *Where Did the Tracks Go.* Saranac Lake, New York: The Chauncey Press, 1985.

Marleau, William R. *Big Moose Station*. Big Moose, New York: Marleau Family Press, 1986.

Marshall, Robert. *Weekend Trips in the Cranberry Lake Region*. Unpublished manuscript, 1923.

McKenney, Clara. "The Cranberry Lake Dam." *The Specter*, March 1947.

Sleicher, Charles Albert. *The Adirondacks: American Playground*. New York: Exposition Press, 1960.

VanValkenburgh, Norman J. *Land Acquisition for New York State*. Arkville, New York: The Catskill Center, 1985.

Other Resources

New York State Department of Enviromental Conservation
  Unit Management Plans for:
Pepperbox Wilderness
Cranberry Lake Wild Forest
Five Ponds Wilderness
Buck Pond and Wanakena Primitive Corridors
  Brochures for:
Bog River Flow
Lake Lila Primitive Area
Stillwater Reservoir

Adirondack Life Articles:
April 1987, "Ponds to Paddle, Rivers to Run" by Mason Smith
December 1988, "The Caretakers" by Christopher Shaw
September 1979, "Nehasane" by Edith Pilcher

Department of Environmental Conservation:
DEC Region 6 Office, Watertown, 315-785-2610
DEC Region 6 Office, Canton, 315-386-4546
DEC Stillwater, Terry Perkins, 315-376-8030

Niagara Mowhawk, pamphlet "Enjoy the great outdoors in Niagara Mohawk country," available at local NIMO offices

Index

Guidebooks from Backcountry Publications

State Parks and Campgrounds
State Parks and Campgrounds in Norther New York, $9.95

Walks and Rambles Series
Walks and Rambles on the Delmarva Peninsula, $8.95
Walks and Rambles in Rhode Island, $8.95
Walks and Rambles in the Upper Connecticut River Valley, $9.95
Walks and Rambles in Westchester (NY) and Fairfield (CT) Counties, $7.95

Biking Series
25 Mountain Bike Tours in Vermont, $9.95
25 Bicycle Tours on Delmarva, $8.95
25 Bicycle Tours in Eastern Pennsylvania, $8.95
20 Bicycle Tours in the Finger Lakes, $7.95
20 Bicycle Tours in the Five Boroughs (NYC), $8.95
25 Bicycle Tours in the Hudson Valley, $9.95
25 Bicycle Tours in Maine, $8.95
25 Bicycle Tours in New Hampshire, $7.95
25 Bicycle Tours in New Jersey, $8.95
20 Bicycle Tours in and around New York City, $7.95
25 Bicycle Tours in Vermont, $8.95

Canoeing Series
Canoe Camping Vermont and New Hampshire Rivers, $7.95
Canoeing Central New York, $10.95
Canoeing Massachusetts, Rhode Island and Connecticut, $7.95

Hiking Series
50 Hikes in the Adirondacks, $10.95
50 Hikes in Central New York, $9.95
50 Hikes in Central Pennsylvania, $9.95
50 Hikes in Connecticut, $10.95
50 Hikes in Eastern Pennsylvania, $10.95
50 Hikes in the Hudson Valley, $9.95
50 Hikes in Massachusetts, $10.95
50 More Hikes in New Hampshire, $9.95

50 Hikes in New Jersey, $10.95
50 Hikes in Northern Maine, $10.95
50 Hikes in Southern Maine, $10.95
50 Hikes in Vermont, $11.95
50 Hikes in West Virginia, $9.95
50 Hikes in Western Pennsylvania,
   $10.95
50 Hikes in the White Mountains, $12.95

Ski-Touring Series
25 Ski Tours in Central New York, $7.95
25 Ski Tours in New Hampshire, $8.95

The above titles are available at bookstores and at certain sporting goods stores or may be ordered directly from the publisher. For complete descriptions of these and other guides, write: The Countryman Press, P.O. Box 175, Woodstock, VT 05091.

Lee M. Brenning, shown here trying out abandoned logging equipment on the trail to High Falls, is an engineering technician at General Electric in Utica, New York. He lives in Nobelboro on the banks of the West Canada Creek. A reverence for the land learned during his youth on his family's farm led him to pursue independent study of local history and the environment. Using his backpacking and bushwhacking skills, Lee explored the Five Ponds Wilderness, the Pepperbox, Lake Lila, and the Bog River for this guide. With his wife, Georgianna, he made many long camping trips into the wilderness and traveled countless miles by foot, canoe, ski, and snowshoe. He also has contributed to three other Discover guides (High Peaks, Southwestern, and West Central). Lee and his wife are deeply involved with forest preserve issues and are active in conservation and recreation organizations.

Peter O'Shea is a retired police sergeant who has become very involved in environmental issues in the north country. He serves on the board of directors of the local Audubon Society and the Indian Creek Nature Center. He has written for *Adirondac* magazine as well as other Adirondack Mountain Club publications. Peter is an avid and knowledgeable student of Adirondack wildlife and is an active member of the New York Chapter of the Wildlife Society. He serves on a subcommittee advising the state on land acquisitions. For this guide Peter concentrated on new trails in the Cranberry Lake area and the new state acquisitions such as Watson's East Triangle and the Diamond-Lassiter lands. He also researched many northern parcels as well as the state forests. Peter is also a contributing author to the *Discover the Northern Adirondacks* guide in this series.